THE NEW LIBRARY
of
THE UNIVERSITY

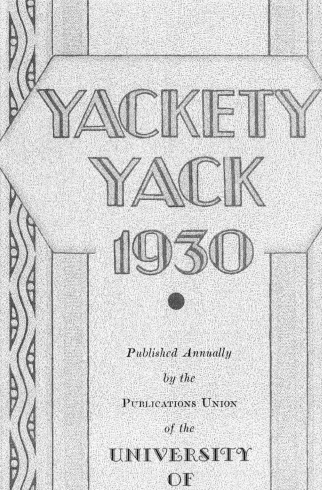

YACKETY YACK

1930

Published Annually

by the

PUBLICATIONS UNION

of the

UNIVERSITY
OF
NORTH
CAROLINA

CHAPEL HILL

VOLUME **XXXX**

ISBN 978-1-332-28752-9
PIBN 10309367

1 MONTH OF
FREE
READING

at

www.ForgottenBooks.com

By purchasing this book you are
eligible for one month membership to
ForgottenBooks.com, giving you
unlimited access to our entire
collection of over 700,000 titles via
our web site and mobile apps.

To claim your free month visit:

www.forgottenbooks.com/free309367

English
Français
Deutsche
Italiano
Español
Português

www.forgottenbooks.com

Mythology Photography **Fiction**
Fishing Christianity **Art** Cooking
Essays Buddhism Freemasonry
Medicine **Biology** Music **Ancient**
Egypt Evolution Carpentry Physics
Dance Geology **Mathematics** Fitness
Shakespeare **Folklore** Yoga Marketing
Confidence Immortality Biographies
Poetry **Psychology** Witchcraft
Electronics Chemistry History **Law**
Accounting **Philosophy** Anthropology
Alchemy Drama Quantum Mechanics
Atheism Sexual Health **Ancient History**
Entrepreneurship Languages Sport
Paleontology Needlework Islam
Metaphysics Investment Archaeology
Parenting Statistics Criminology
Motivational

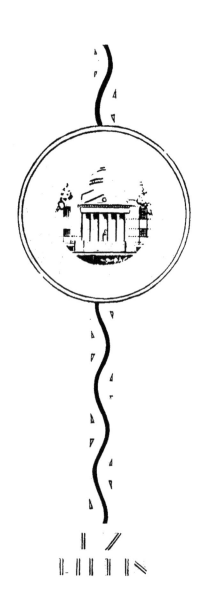

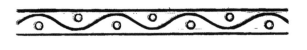

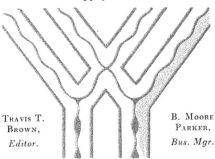

TRAVIS T.
BROWN,
Editor.

B. MOORE
PARKER,
Bus. Mgr.

YACKE
WA

TRAVIS TAYLOR BROWN,
Editor-in-Chief.

B. MOORE PARKER,
Business Manager.

HARRY JOSEPH GALLAND,
Associate Editor.

ROBERT LEE GRAHAM,
Associate Editor.

ROBERT MAYNE ALBRIGHT,
Assistant Editor.

WILLIAM CLYDE DUNN,
Assistant Editor.

CLAUDE HERMAN FARRELL,
Assistant Business Manager.

THROUGH the years, books inform and entertain us. Some, the records of experiences and adventures, serve as reminders. Such a book, we, the editors of the YACKETY-YACK of 1930, present to you.

It is but a link in a long and honorable chain, composed of the yearbooks of the past. To forge this latest link as strong as its predecessors has not been an easy task. Its strength, judged by the success with which it recalls the college years, we leave to you.

In keeping with the Renaissance of the South in the literary world, the theme of the Annual has been centered around the new Library of the University. As literature records the experiences and adventures of life, so we hope this volume will record successfully for you the experiences and adventures of your years at Carolina.

ARCHIBALD HENDERSON, Ph.D., D.C.L., LL.D.

As the University of North Carolina, hardly known outside the State in the nineteenth century, achieved a European vogue in the twentieth through Archibald Henderson's activity as a specialist in modern dramaturgy, and incidentally as my friend and biographer, I embrace the opportunity with which I have been honored of dedicating this 1930 Yackety Yack to him

G. Bernard Shaw

IN MEMORIAM

PHILIP HENRY ATKINSON, '27
ASHEVILLE, N. C.
1904-1929

PAUL S. FOSTER, '28
ASHEVILLE, N. C.
1904-1929

HARVEY L. HALL, '29
GOLDSBORO, N. C.
1906-1929

SEATON GALES LINDSAY, JR., '30
DURHAM, N. C.
1909-1929

HENRY B. MCNAIR, JR., '27
TARBORO, N. C.
1904-1929

WALLACE A. SMITH, '27
RALEIGH, N. C.
1905-1929

THE
UNIVERSITY

John Henry Newman

CARDINAL NEWMAN

The University educates the intellect to reason well in all matters, to reach out toward the truth and to grasp it.

—IDEA OF A UNIVERSITY.

GLIMPSES
OF CAROLINA

FACULTY

Francis Bacon

BACON

Who taught the parrot its good morrow?

—Essays.

HARRY WOODBURN CHASE, PH.D., LL.D.

THE PRESIDENT'S MESSAGE

I hope that this book will serve for many a year to arouse pleasant memories of the life at Carolina. The years here are so bound up with hopes and aspirations, joys and ambitions, that they will always stand out as among the happiest in your lives. This book is a visible symbol of these years, and as such it will play its part in many a happy hour of recollection. To all of you who are included within its pages, and especially to those of you who are graduating from the University this year, I wish good fortune and happiness from your alma mater.

H. W. CHASE, *President.*

ADDISON
HIBBARD, M.A.

*Dean of the
College of
Liberal Arts.*

JAMES
MUNSIE
BELL, Ph.D.

*Acting-Dean
of the School of
Applied Science.*

GUSTAVE
MAURICE
BRAUNE, C.E.

*Dean of the
School of
Engineering.*

CHARLES
TILFORD
McCORMICK, A.B., L.L.B

*Dean of the
School of
Law.*

DUDLEY
DeWITT
CARROLL, M.A.

*Dean of the
School of
Commerce.*

JAMES
FINCH
ROYSTER, Ph.D.

*Dean of the
Graduate
School.*

NATHAN
WILSON
WALKER, Ed.M.

*Acting-Dean of
the School of
Education and
Director of the
Summer School.*

ISAAC
HALL
MANNING, M.D.

*Dean of the
School of
Medicine.*

EDWARD
VERNON
HOWELL, A.B., Ph.G.

*Dean of the
School of
Pharmacy.*

HOWARD
WASHINGTON
ODUM, Ph.D.

*Director of
the School
of Public
Welfare and
of the Institute
for Research in
Social Science.*

CLASSES

Jean Jacques Rousseau

ROUSSEAU

And if your student knows the people around him, he will find his place in the world.

—EMILE.

The Search Ends.

SENIORS

YACKETY YACK

Officers of the Senior Class

RALPH C. GREENE..President
DAVID NIMS...Vice-President
W. B. MORGAN...Secretary
BEATTY RECTOR...Treasurer
ROBERT GRAHAM...Representative on Student Council

Class Day Officers

BOB GRAHAM		BILL BOBBITT
Lawyer		*Statistician*
	JOHN MEBANE	
	Poet	
JOHNSON ALEXANDER		CY EDSON
Historian		*Prophet*

Executive Committee

FLEMING WILY, *Chairman*   A. A. SEAWELL
S. S. McNEELY, JR.   ROGER WALKER
ROBERT ZEALY   HARRY GALLAND
ROSS PORTER   ARCHIE ALLEN
GORDON GRAY   JOHNSON ALEXANDER
J. C. WILLIAMS

HAROLD I. AARON

SPENCER, N. C.

Age: 21   Degree: B.S. Commerce

Δ Σ Π

WILLIAM JACKSON ADAMS

CARTHAGE, N. C.

Age: 21   Degree: A.B.

Woodberry Forest Club; Student Entertainment Committee; Dialetic Senate; Ball Manager; Yackety Yack Staff, (1, 2); Buccaneer Staff, (1, 2); Amphoterothen; Coop; German Club; Vice-President Phi Beta Kappa.

Φ Κ Σ, Φ Β Κ

GEORGE ZACHARIAL ALDEN

ARDEN, N. C.

Age: 25   Degree: A.B. Education

JOHN JOHNSTON ALEXANDER

CHARLOTTE, N. C.

Age: 21   Degree: B.S. Elec. Engineering

Freshman Track; Senior Executive Committee; Δ. I. E. E., (1, 2, 3); President A. I. E. E., (4); Junior-Senior Y. Cabinet, (4); Inter-fraternity Council; Manager Cross Country, (4); Manager Track, (4).

Θ Χ, Φ Ζ Ν

PENELOPE ALEXANDER

CHARLOTTE, N. C.

Age: 19   Degree: A.B.

Playmakers.

Δ Δ Δ

ARCH TURNER ALLEN, JR.

RALEIGH, N. C.

Age: 19   Degree: B.S.; C.E.

Gorgon's Head; Minotaurs; President Athletic Association; Treasurer Junior Class; Senior Class Executive Committee; Boxing Team, (2, 3); Captain Boxing Team. (4); Gabin; German Club; Commencement Marshall; Ball Manager; Monogram Club.

Σ N

JOHN HUSKE ANDERSON, JR.

FAYETTEVILLE, N. C.

Age: 22   Degree: LL.B.

Tar Heel Ed. Staff, (1, 2); Vice-Pres. Freshman "Y" Cabinet; Sophomore Y. M. C. A. Cabinet; Junior-Senior Y. M. C. A. Cabinet; Grail, Asst. Treas. (3); Treas. of Grail, (4); Phi Assembly; Amphoterothen; Gorgon's Head; Asst. Leader of Junior Prom; Asst. Leader of Mid-Winter Dances, (4); Ed. Board of the N. C. Law Review, (4); Asst. Ed. of Law Review, Research Asst. of Law School.

B Θ Π, Φ Δ Φ

LACY ALLEN ANDREW, JR.

GREENSBORO, N. C.

Age: 22   Degree: B.S. Medicine

Elisha Mitchell Scientific Society; North Carolina Medical Society; Secretary-Treasurer of First Year Medical Class; Botany Assistant; Freshman Wrestling; Dormitory Club.

Λ Κ Κ

DAVID LEONARD AVNER

MORGANTOWN, W. VA.

Age: 22   Degree: A.B.

Playmakers; Wigue and Masque; Deutsche Verein;
Inter-fraternity Council.

Z B T

EDWIN BURTIS AYCOCK

FREMONT, N. C.

Age: 20   Degree: A.B.

Freshman Baseball Squad, (1); Sub-Assistant Mana-
ger of Basketball, (2); University Little Symphony
Orchestra, (1, 2, 3, 4); University Band, (2, 3, 4);
Dormitory Club, (4).

EDWIN OSBORNE AYSCUE

MONROE, N. C.

Age: 25   Degree: LL.B.

HENRY McKEAN BAGGS

WASHINGTON, D. C.

Age: 21   Degree: A.B.

X Ψ

DAVID GRAHAM BALL
RALEIGH, N. C.
Age: 21   Degree: B.S. Commerce

ALICE CAROLYN BALLENGER
WELLFORD, S. C.
Age: 20   Degree: A.B.

CHARLES WHITLOCK BANNER
GREENSBORO, N. C.
Age: 21   Degree: B.S. Commerce
Freshman Friendship Council; Freshman Wrestling;
Y. M. C. A. Cabinet; Wrestling Squad, (1); Ger-
man Club; Woodberry Forest Club.
Π Κ Φ, Ε Φ Δ, Α Κ Ψ, Φ Β Κ

ELIZABETH SWANN BARBER
RALEIGH, N. C.
Age: 21   Degree: A.B.
Carolina Playmakers; Wigue and Masque; Woman's
Association.
Π Β Φ

MINOR BARKLEY

STATESVILLE, N. C.

Age: 22   Degree: A.B. Education

Captain Freshman Cross Country; Captain Varsity
Cross Country, (4); Track, (2, 3, 4).

RAYMOND ELMO BASS

BLACK CREEK, N. C.

Age: 21   Degree: B.S. Chemistry

Λ Χ Σ

HELEN LOUISE BAYLOR

KNOXVILLE, TENN.

Age: 24   Degree: A.B. Education

HENRY CLAY BELL

BESSEMER CITY, N. C.

Age: 22   Degree: Ph.G.

WILLIAM OTIS BENNETT
WARREN, PA.
Age: 21   Degree: A.B.
Χ Ψ

CARL WALTER BLACKWOOD
MELVIN HILL, N. C.
Age: 24   Degree: A.B. Education
Σ Ε

WILLIAM EDGAR BOBBITT
ROCKY MOUNT, N. C.
Age: 21   Degree: B.S. Civil Engineering
Art Editor of Buccaneer. (2, 3); A. S. C. E.
Π Κ Φ, Τ Β Π

HARRY EUGENE BOLEN
DANVILLE, VA.
Age: 21   Degree: B.S. Pharmacy
American Pharmaceutical Association; Student Coun-
cil, (3, 4); Elisha Mitchell Scientific Society.
Φ Δ Χ, Ρ Χ

GEORGE WASHINGTON BRADHAM
NEW BERN, N. C.
Age: 22   Degree: A.B.
B Θ Π

HARRY GRAY BRAINARD
SPENCERPORT, NEW YORK
Age: 22   Degree: B.S. Commerce
Business Staff of Buccaneer, (2, 3); Y. M. C. A.
Cabinet.
Σ Δ, Δ Σ Π

JOHN BRANDT
CHAPEL HILL, N. C.
Age: 21   Degree: A.B.
Cabin.
Δ Ψ

DANIEL JOHNSON BRAWLEY
STATESVILLE, N. C.
Age: 22   Degree: B.S. Chemistry
A X Σ

I. STANLEY BREIT

NEW YORK, N. Y.

Age: 22   Degree: A.B. Education

SIDNEY BRICK

DILLON, S. C.

Age: 21   Degree: B.S. Commerce

Tar Heel Business Staff, (3. 4); Yackety Yack Business Staff, (4).

Φ Λ

JOSEPH HERMAN BRISSON

ST. PAULS, N. C.

Age: 22   Degree: A.B. Education

Σ Z

BENJAMIN THORP BRODIE

HENDERSON, N. C.

Age: 20   Degree: A.B.

Sophomore Y. M. C. A. Cabinet.

BERTRAM HOOLE BROWN

TARBORO, N. C.

Age: 22   Degree: A.B.

Inter-fraternity Council.

Φ Γ Δ

HAZEL LANDRETH BROWN

STATESVILLE, N. C.

Age: 20   Degree: A.B.

TRAVIS TAYLOR BROWN

CHARLOTTE, N. C.

Age: 21   Degree: A.B.

Freshman Friendship Council; Vice-President of
Sophomore "Y" Cabinet; Phi Assembly; Yackety
Yack Staff, (1, 2, 3); Editor-in-chief, (4); Varsity
Track Squad; Publications Union Board; Ampho-
terothen; Grail; Coop; Golden . Fleece; Executive
Committee of German Club.

Φ Γ Δ, Φ Δ Φ, Ε Φ Δ, Φ Β Κ

WILLIAM HOWARD BROWN

GREENVILLE, N. C.

Age: 19   Degree: A.B.

Freshman Basketball; Varsity Basketball; Phi
Assembly.

Δ Σ Φ

John Henry Brunjes, Jr.
WILMINGTON, N. C.

Age: 21   Degree: A.B.

Band, (1, 2, 3); President of Band, (4); Freshman Tennis.

Σ Φ Σ

William Clingan Burnett
TRYON, N. C.

Age: 21   Degree: B.S. Elec. Engineering

Cheerios, (1); American Institute of Electrical Engineers; Secretary, (2); Treasurer, (2); Taylor Society; President, (4); Dialetic Senate.

Θ Φ, Φ Z N

Edward Purnell Cahoon
COLUMBIA, N. C.

Age: 26   Degree: Ph.G. Pharmacy

Φ Δ Χ

Newton Sudduth Calhoun
WINSTON-SALEM, N. C.

Age: 20   Degree: B.S. Commerce

Z Ψ

CHARLIE CARROLL CARPENTER

CHERRYVILLE, N. C.

Age: 21   Degree: A.B. Education

Wrestling Squad.

MARY LEWISE CARPENTER

DALLAS, TEXAS

Age: 21   Degree: A.B.

Π Β Φ

FREDERICK LOUIS CARR, JR.

WILSON, N. C.

Age: 20   Degree: A.B.

Coop; "13" Club; Phi Assembly; Sub-Assistant Manager Football; Assistant Business Manager- Buccaneer; Leader Junior Prom; Commencement Ball Manager; Senior Order of Daviens.

Σ Ν

GABRIEL PAUL CARR

TEACHEYS, N. C.

Age: 22   Degree: A.B.

Τ Κ Α

WILLIAM GRAY CARR

WILSON, N. C.

Age: 20   Degree: B.S. Commerce

Κ Α

CLARENCE COLEMAN CATES

BURLINGTON, N. C.

Age: 22   Degree: A.B.

Φ Β Κ

1930

WILLIAM CHURCHILL CHEATHAM

RALEIGH, N. C.

Age: 20   Degree: B.S. Commerce

Cabin; Gorgon's Head; Freshman Football Squad; Freshman Baseball Squad.

Σ Α Ε

NELLE RIVES CHEEK

CHAPEL HILL, N. C.

Age: 24   Degree: A.B.

HUBERT LEE CLAPP

SWANNANOA, N. C.

Age: 23   Degree: B.S. Medicine

Elisha Mitchell Scientific Society.

Δ K K

CHRISTINE L. COFFEY

LEWISBURG, TENNESSEE

Age: 19   Degree: A.B.

GABRIEL MURREL COHEN

LOUISVILLE, KY.

Age: 21   Degree: A.B.

Tar Heel; Varsity Track; Varsity Cross Country.

Φ Δ

GEORGE FREDERIC COLE

SOUTHERN PINES, N. C.

Age: 24   Degree: A.B. Education

President Cercle Francais, (3).

BETH COLLEY

BLOOMSBURG, PA.

Age: 22   Degree: A.B.

Playmakers.

RALPH STOKES COLLINS

AYDEN, N. C.

Age: 19   Degree: A.B.

Φ B K

JOHN WOLTZ COMER

DOBSON, N. C.

Age: 29   Degree: A.B. Education

Acacia.

GEORGE LESLIE CONLEY

MARION, N. C.

Age: 21   Degree: B.S. Commerce

Δ Σ Π

AUGUSTUS MCALISTER COVINGTON

TATUM, S. C.

Age: 24   Degree: A.B., LL.B.

Mary D. Wright Debate, (2); Phi Society; Sergeant-at-Arms, (3); President Dormitory Club, (4); Summer School Student Council, (4); President, ('5); Inter-fraternity Council, (5, 6).

Σ Z, Δ Θ Φ

DAVID JENKINS CRAIG, JR.

CHARLOTTE, N. C.

Age: 22   Degree: A.B.

Minotaurs; Gorgon's Head; Manager Football; German Club.

Δ K E   Φ Δ Φ

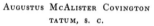

JOHN THOMAS CRAIG

CHARLOTTE, N. C.

Age: 19   Degree: A.B.

Δ K E

GEORGE EDWARD CRAWLY

ESSEX, N. C.

Age: 22   Degree: A.B. Education

LILLIAN BEATRICE CRISFIELD
CHARLOTTE, N. C.
Age: 20   Degree: A.B.

ANNE KELSO CURRIE
FAYETTEVILLE, N. C.
Age: 20   Degree: A.B. Education
Wigue and Masque.

Π Β Φ

SYDNEY McLEAN CURRY
RALEIGH, N. C.
Age: 20   Degree: A.B. Education
Χ Ω

WILLIAM RANDOLPH CURTIS
FRANKLINVILLE, N. C.
Age: 20   Degree: A.B.
Φ Β Κ

CHARLES CLAXTON DALTON
FOREST CITY, N. C.
Age: 23   Degree: A.B. Education

CYRUS ROBERT DAVIS
FULTON, N. Y.
Age: 23   Degree: B.S. Civil Engineering
American Society of Civil Engineers.

ELMER ROBERT DAVIS
SOUTHERN PINES, N. C.
Age: 21   Degree: B.S. Elec. Engineering
Freshman Track; Freshman Cross Country; American Institute of Electrical Engineers.
A Λ T

ELBERT HUBBARD DENNING
ALBEMARLE, N. C.
Age: 21   Degree: A.B. Journalism
Tar Heel Staff, (3); City Editor, (4); Rifle Club, (2, 3); Secretary Rifle Club, (4); Rifle Team.
Φ Σ Κ

SUZANNE T. DENT
LOCKHART, S. C.
Age: 21   Degree: **A.B.**
House President of Spencer Hall.
Λ Γ Δ

PAUL WILLIAM DONELLY
SUTHERLAND, N. C.
Age: 23   Degree: A.B. Education
Acacia.

FRANCIS ELMER DRAKE
SCOTLAND NECK, N. C.
Age: 21   Degree: B.S. Elec. Engineering
Φ Z N

FRED BROWN DRAKE
HENDERSONVILLE, N. C.
Age: 22   Degree: B.S. Commerce

WILLIAM HENRY DRY
CARY, N. C.
Age: 21   Degree: B.S. Commerce
Buccaneer Art Staff, (1, 2, 3); Freshman Track
Team; Varsity Track Squad (2, 3, 4).
Θ Φ

MARY MARSHALL DUNLAP
ROXBORO, N. C.
Age: 19   Degree: A.B.

CELESTE EDGERTON
KENLY, N. C.
Age: 20   Degree: A.B.
Wigue and Masque; Woman's Association.
Π Β Φ

CYRUS MELVIN EDSON
TAMPA, FLA.
Age: 21   Degree: A.B. Education
Buccaneer Staff, (3); Editor of Buccaneer, (4);
Playmakers, (3, 4); Di Senate, (3, 4); North Caro-
lina Collegiate Press Association, (4); Y. M. C. A.
Cabinet, (3).
Χ Φ

RUFUS ROBERT EDWARDS

FALCON, N. C.

Age: 22   Degree: A.B. Education

THOMAS HICKS EDWARDS

RUTHERFORDTON, N. C.

Age: 21   Degree: A.B. Education

Freshman Baseball; Varsity Baseball, (3, 4); Boxing Squad.

JANE JEANNETTE ERNST

CHAPEL HILL, N. C.

Age: 20   Degree: A.B.

Φ M

WALTER EUGENE ESKEW

GREENVILLE, S. C.

Age: 20   Degree: B.S. Chem. Engineering

Varsity Football, (2, 3, 4); Monogram Club; German Club.

X Φ

JOHN HERBERT ESTEP
WHITEHEAD, N. C.
Age: 21   Degree: A.B.
Glee Club. (2); Fencing Team. (3, 4).
E Φ Δ

LYDA HARRIS EUBANKS
CHAPEL HILL, N. C.
Age: 20   Degree: A.B. Education

ERNEST WYTTENBACH EWBANK
HENDERSONVILLE, N. C.
Age: 19   Degree: A.B.
The Cabin; Winner of Grail Intra-mural Cup.
Φ Δ Θ

SARA GILMOUR FALKENER
GOLDSBORO, N. C.
Age: 19   Degree: A.B. Education
Π Β Φ

STUART ALLAN FARLEIGH
CHICAGO, ILL.
Age: 22   Degree: A.B.
Freshman Basketball; Freshman Baseball; Cabin;
German Club; Varsity Basketball; Yackety Yack;
Business Staff, (3); Blue Key Society; Tar Heel
Staff, (1).

Σ Λ E

RAY SIMPSON FARRIS
CHARLOTTE, N. C.
Age: 22   Degree: B.S. Commerce
Secretary of Freshman Class; Freshman Football;
Captain Freshman Boxing; Varsity Football, (2, 3);
Captain Varsity Football, (4); Varsity Baseball, (2);
President of Junior Class; President of Student
Body; Golden Fleece: Grail; Daviens; Dialetic
Senate.

Σ Φ Σ

JULIAN BAKER FENNER
TARBORO, N. C.
Age: 21   Degree: A.B.
Freshman Football; Varsity Football, (2, 3, 4);
Monogram Club; Freshman Basketball; Varsity
Basketball, (2, 3).

Δ K E

FRANK REAVIS FLEMING
HAMPTONVILLE, N. C.
Age: 23   Degree: A.B. Education
Baseball; Monogram Club.

[50]

MARION GEDDINGS FOLLIN, JR.

WINSTON-SALEM, N. C.

Age: 21   Degree: B.S. Commerce

Y. M. C. A. Cabinet; Dialetic Senate; Commencement Marshal; Thirteen Club; German Club; Gimghouls; Grail; Senior Order of Daviens.

Β Θ Π, Α Κ Ψ

DOROTHY FOOSHE

NEW YORK, N. Y.

Age: 20   Degree: A.B.

Χ Ω

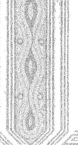

JOHN FRED FORD

BELMONT, N. C.

Age: 21   Degree: B.S. Commerce

Inter-fraternity Council; German Club.

Σ Φ Σ

MAURINE FORESTER

DALLAS, TEXAS

Age: 21   Degree: A.B.

Woman's Association; Wigue and Masque.

Π Β Φ

JOSEPH THOMAS FOWLER

CHAPEL HILL, N. C.

Age: 21   Degree: B.S. Commerce

HARRY JOSEPH GALLAND

BROOKLYN, N. Y.

Age: 21   Degree: A.B.
Tar Heel Reporter, (1); Asst. Ed., (2); Associate
Ed., (3, 4); Buccaneer Staff; Yackety Yack Ed.
Staff: Asst. Ed., (4); Mary D. Wright Debate;
Dialetic Senate; Manager Fencing Team, (3, 4);
Publicity Director of "Mum's the Word"; Wigue and
Masque; Rifle Club and Team; Publications Union
Board; Senior Class Ex. Com.; Amphoterothen;
            Grail; Golden Fleece.

Z B T, E Φ Δ

WILLIAM IRVING GARRIS

MURFREESBORO, N. C.

Age: 23   Degree: A.B. Education

ALFRED WADDELL GHOLSON, JR.

HENDERSON, N. C.

Age: 22   Degree: LL.B.

Freshman Friendship Council; Gym Instructor;
Monogram Club; Inter-fraternity Council, Secre-
tary and Treasurer; Secretary and Treasurer Second
Year Law Class; Law Review; President Law
            School Association.

Π Κ Φ, Φ Δ Φ, E Φ Δ

HARRY MARION GILBERT
DARLINGTON, S. C.
Age: 21   Degree: A.B.
Λ Λ Τ

GEORGE BROWNE GOODE
RUTHERFORD COLLEGE, N. C.
Age: 23   Degree: B.S. Commerce
Y. M. C. A. Cabinet.
Σ Ε

ELSIE SWINK GRADY
KENLY, N. C.
Age: 17   Degree: A.B.
Σ Τ Χ

ROBERT LEE GRAHAM, JR.
CHARLOTTE, N. C.
Age: 20   Degree: A.B.
Vice-President Freshman Friendship Council; Y. M.
C. A. Cabinet; Phi Assembly; Cabin; German Club;
Assistant Editor Yackety Yack; Amphoterothen;
Senior Class Executive Committee; Student Council
Representative Senior Class.
Φ Γ Δ, Φ Β Κ

WILLIAM EDWARD GRANT
WINSTON-SALEM, N. C.

Age: 23   Degree: A.B.

CALVIN GRAVES, JR.
MOUNT AIRY, N. C.

Age: 20   Degree: A.B.
Senior Order of Daviens; Tar Heel; Mary D.
Wright Debate.

Π Κ Φ, Ε Φ Δ, Φ Δ Φ

GORDON GRAY
WINSTON-SALEM, N. C.

Age: 20   Degree: A.B.
Minotaurs; Gimghouls; Daviens; Golden Fleece;
President Phi Beta Kappa; Manager Varsity Base-
ball; Business Manager Magazine; Commencement
Marshal; Class Executive Committee, (2, 3, 4);
German Club Executive .Committee.

Δ Κ Ε, Α Ψ Δ, Φ Β Κ

ALTON GLENN GREENE
CANDOR, N. C.

Age: 23   Degree: A.B. Education
North Carolina Club.

RALPH CORDELL GREENE

MARSHVILLE, N. C.

Age: 20   Degree: B.S. Commerce

President of Senior Class; Assistant Manager of
Basketball; Manager Freshman Basketball; Y. M.
C. A. Cabinet, (1, 2, 3, 4); Treasurer, (2); Treasurer
of Grail; Dialetic Senate; Student Council, (3);
Business Staff of Yackety Yack; Assistant Leader of
Junior Prom; German Club; Order of the Daviens;
Golden Fleece.

Σ Z, Φ B K

STANLEY EVERETTE GREEN

BOILING SPRINGS, N. C.

Age: 23   Degree: A.B. Education

Glee Club; Vice-President of Cleveland County
Club; Y. M. C. A. Cabinet, (3).

THOMAS EDMOND GRIFFIN

MONROE, N. C.

Age: 21   Degree: A.B.

GEORGE WINSTON HAMER

MC COLL, S. C.

Age: 20   Degree: A.B.

Cabin; Track Squad; Inter-fraternity Council.

Σ N

JASON HUGH HARDIN

FOREST CITY, N. C.

Age: 21   Degree: A.B. Education

JAMES TURNER HARDEN

GRAHAM, N. C.

Age: 23   Degree: A.B. Education

Freshman Football; Varsity Football, (3, 4); Freshman Baseball; Varsity Baseball, (2, 3); Monogram Club.

PHOEBE RANDOLPH HARDING

WASHINGTON, N. C.

Age: 20   Degree: A.B. Education

Secretary Woman's Association, (4); Playmakers, (4); Wigue and Masque.

Π B Φ

SANFORD C. HARPER, JR.

WINSTON-SALEM, N. C.

Age: 20   Degree: B.S. Commerce

Σ Φ E

LINWOOD PARKER HARRELL
EDENTON, N. C.
Age: 22   Degree: B.S. Commerce
Σ E

BOYD WHITE HARRIS, JR.
DURHAM, N. C.
Age: 22   Degree: B.S. Commerce
Δ Σ Π

THASSEUS VALMONTE HEDGPETH
ELM CITY, N. C.
Age: 21   Degree: B.S. Elec. Engineering
German Club; Cabin; Vice-President of A. I. E. E.;
Taylor Society.
Σ N, T B Π, Φ Z N

WILLIAM LOGAN HIGDON, JR.
FRANKLIN, N. C.
Age: 19   Degree: B.S. Commerce
Wrestling Squad.
Δ Σ Π

H. Osborne Hill

CHERRYVILLE, N. C.

Age: 20   Degree: B.S. Civil Engineering
American Society of Civil Engineers.

Conrad Ogburn Hinshaw

PLEASANT GARDEN, N. C.

Age: 23   Degree: A.B. Education

John Irving Hocutt

CLAYTON, N. C.

Age: 24   Degree: A.B. Education

Glenn Parran Holder

GREENSBORO, N. C.

Age: 24   Degree: A.B.

Editor Daily Tar Heel, (4); Golden Fleece; Amphoterothen; Magazine; Class Executive Committee, (1, 3); Managing Editor, Associate Editor Tar Heel, (3); Reporter Tar Heel, (1, 2); Secretary Publications Union Board, (3); Senior Order of Daviens; Alumni Review.

Σ Δ, Ε Φ Δ

LEONARD HOWLETT HOLE

GREENSBORO, N. C.

Age: 22   Degree: A.B.

Di Senate: Inter-fraternity Council, (3); "Kalif of Kavak," (2); Woodberry Forest Club; Blue Key Society; German Club; Assistant Sophomore Hop, (2); Chief Commencement Ball Manager, (4).

Σ Χ, Σ Τ

WILLIAM ROBERT HOOKS

FREMONT, N. C.

Age: 21   Degree: A.B.

WILLIAM JOHNSTON HORNEY, JR.

GREENSBORO, N. C.

Age: 23   Degree: B.S. Civil Engineering

American Society of Civil Engineers.

Σ Δ

ERNEST ESTES HOUSE

GRAND FORKS, NORTH DAKOTA

Age: 22   Degree: A.B.

Σ Ν

FRANCIS MARION HOUSTON

RALEIGH, N. C.

Age: 20   Degree: B.S. Commerce

Π K A

ROBERT ALEXANDER HOVIS

CHARLOTTE, N. C.

Age: 21   Degree: A.B.

Glee Club, (1, 2, 3, 4); Y. M. C. A. Cabinet, (2); Yackety Yack Staff, (1, 2); Assistant Editor Yackety Yack, (3); German Club; Executive Committee Junior Class.

X Ψ, Φ M A, Φ B K

CAMERON CHRISTOPHER HOWARD

DEEP RUN, N. C.

Age: 25   Degree: B.S. Civil Engineering

American Society of Civil Engineers.

HUGHES BAYNE HOYLE, JR.

MANTEO, N. C.

Age: 20   Degree: A.B. Education

North Carolina Academy of Science; Mathematics Club.

WALTER HOYLE
LINCOLNTON, N. C.
Age: 24   Degree: A.B., LL.B.
Law Review.
Π Κ Φ, Φ Δ Φ, Π Δ Ε, Α Δ Σ

WILLIAM BEEKMAN HUGER
SAVANNAH, GA.
Age: 23   Degree: A.B.
Gimghouls; Coop.
Σ Α Ε

PAUL ADDISON HUNT
PLEASANT GARDEN, N. C.
Age: 20   Degree: B.S. Commerce

SHELTON BRINSON HUNTER
MAGNOLIA, N. C.
Age: 21   Degree: A.B.
Θ Κ Ν

Thomas Allison Hunter

GREENSBORO, N. C.

Age: 21   Degree: A.B.

Freshman Friendship Council; Assistant Manager
Wrestling; Assistant Leader Junior Prom; Commencement Ball Manager.

Σ X

Thomas Lindsay Hunter

LINCOLNTON, N. C.

Age: 22   Degree: A.B. Education

1930

Addie Currier Huske

FAYETTEVILLE, N. C.

Age: 26   Degree: A.B. Education

Isaac Hall Huske

FAYETTEVILLE, N. C.

Age: 21   Degree: A.B.

Senior Order of Daviens; Y. M. C. A. Cabinet.

X Φ

JOHN ROBERT INGRAM, JR.

SANFORD, N. C.

Age: 22   Degree: B.S. Commerce

Θ X

WILLIAM THOMAS JACKSON, JR.

WEEKSVILLE, N. C.

Age: 21   Degree: B.S. Commerce

Φ Σ K

AUGUSTUS HENRY JARRATT, JR.
CONCORD, N. C.
Age: 21   Degree: A.B.
German Club.
Σ X

BURT POWERS JOHNSON
LILLINGTON, N. C.
Age: 20   Degree: A.B.

ELIZABETH JOHNSON
LOUISBURG, N. C.
Age: 20   Degree: A.B.
Editorial Staff of Tar Heel.

HENRY LIVINGSTON JOHNSON
DILLON, S. C.
Age: 22   Degree: A.B.

WILLIAM ROBERT JOHNSON

FOUR OAKS, N. C.

Age: 22   Degree: A.B. Education

FRANK ALLEN JONES

COFIELD, N. C.

Age: 20   Degree: A.B. Education

Θ Κ Ν

JACOB SIDNEY KIRK

MOCKSVILLE, N. C.

Age: 20   Degree: B.S. Elec. Engineering

American Institute of Electrical Engineers.

Δ Φ

WILLIAM SMITH KOENIG

GREENSBORO, N. C.

Age: 21   Degree: A.B.

Varsity Football, (2, 3, 4); Vice-President of Monogram Club; Sophomore Order of Sheiks; Freshman
Football; Freshman Boxing; Freshman Track.

Δ Κ Ε

FRANKLIN BANKS KUYKENDAL, JR.

MATTHEWS, N. C.

Age: 24   Degree: B.S. Elec. Engineering

T B Π, Φ B K, Φ Z N

EDITH ELIZABETH KYLES

STATESVILLE, N. C.

Age: 20   Degree: A.B.

DEWEY WINFRED LAMBERT

GREENSBORO, N. C.

Age: 21   Degree: B.S. Commerce

JOHN ALBERT LANG

CARTHAGE, N. C.

Age: 19   Degree: A.B.

President of the Philanthropic Assembly, (4); Vice-
President of the Y.M.C.A., (4); Y.M.C.A. Cabinet,
(1, 2, 3, 4); Inter-collegiate Debater; Carolina Playmakers; Deutsche Verein.

E Φ Δ, Φ K Δ, Φ B K

MOSES DOW LASITTER, JR.

GREENVILLE, N. C.

Age: 21   Degree: B.S. Commerce

Δ Σ Π

CHARLES MERITT LEAR

CHAPEL HILL, N. C.

Age: 22   Degree: B.S. Elec. Engineering

American Institute of Electrical Engineers; Taylor
Society.

Θ Φ, Φ Z N

CHARLES McIVER LEDBETTER

DOME, N. C.

Age: 24   Degree: B.S. Civil Engineering

GEORGE WESLEY LEWIS

MARSHALLBERG, N. C.

Age: 23   Degree: A.B. Education

LEONARD DANIEL LEWIS

HENDERSONVILLE, N. C.

Age: 20   Degree: B.S. Commerce

Carolina Playmakers; Tar Heel Staff.

Φ A

LUTHER M. LEWIS

JAISON, N. C.

Age: 22   Degree: A.B. Education

THOMAS ANTHONY LIBBUS

NEW BERN, N. C.

Age: 24   Degree: B.S. Pharmacy

American Pharmaceutical Association.

Φ Δ X, E Φ Δ, P X

JOHN VAN LINDLEY

GREENSBORO, N. C.

Age: 21   Degree: A.B.

Sheiks; German Club; Gimghoul; Asst. Manager of Football.

Δ K E

J. BIRNEY LINN

NEEDHAM, MASS.

Age: 26   Degree: LL.B.

Y. M. C. A. Cabinet; Pan-Hellenic Council;. Sub-
Assistant Manager of Baseball; Assistant Manager
of Baseball; Manager of Freshman Baseball; Dialectic Senate.

Σ Φ Ε, Φ Α Δ

JAMES THOMPSON LOHNES, JR.

VALLEY FALLS, N. Y.

Age: 19   Degree: A.B.

German Club.

Θ Δ Χ

KERMOT LOHR

LEXINGTON, N. C.

Age: 19   Degree: B.S. Medicine

Davidson County Club.

Σ Ε

GEORGE ATTMORE LONG

GRAHAM, N. C.

Age: 19   Degree: A.B.

Φ Β Κ

· GEORGE W. LOVE

HORSE SHOE, N. C.

Age: 18   Degree: A.B. Education

EDWIN LAWRENCE LOWERY

WINGATE, N. C.

Age: 20   Degree: B.S. Mech. Engineering
President of Student Branch of American Society
of Mechanical Engineers; Taylor Society.

ROY FRANK LOWRY

HICKORY, VIRGINIA

Age: 22   · Degree: A.B. Education
Freshman Track; Varsity Track

Φ K Δ

WALTER GUINN LOWRY, JR.

PINEVILLE, N. C.

Age: 21   Degree: A.B.

Freshman Basketball; Freshman Cross Country;
Freshman Track; Varsity Track, (2, 3, 4); Cross
Country; Monogram Club.

NAPOLEON B. LUFTY

GREENSBORO, N. C.

Age: 20   Degree: A.B.

Freshman Friendship Council; Sophomore Y.M.C.A. Cabinet; Junior-Senior Cabinet; Varsity Baseball, (2, 4); Captain Varsity Baseball, (3); Monogram Club; Varsity Basketball Squad, (3); Sub-Assistant Manager of Wrestling, (2); Inter-dormitory Council, (2, 3).

Θ K N

HOMER LeGRAND LYON, JR.

WHITEVILLE, N. C.

Age: 22   Degree: A.B.

"13" Club; German Club; Glee Club, (1, 2, 3, 4); Business Manager of Glee Club, (4).

Z Ψ, Φ M A

WILLIAM HERBERT McCALL

MURPHY, N. C.

Age: 21   Degree: A.B.

Θ Φ

DeWITT CLINTON McCOTTER, JR.

CASH CORNER, N. C.

Age: 20   Degree: B.S. Commerce

Cabin; German Club.

Φ Γ Δ, A K Ψ

DANIEL RICHARD McGLOHON
WINTON, N. C.
Age: 22   Degree: A.B.
Freshman Boxing Team; Band, (1, 2, 3); Tar Heel
Staff, (2, 3); German Club.

RAYMOND LEE McHARGUE
STATESVILLE, N. C.
Age: 21   Degree: A.B. Education

EARNEST CLEWELL McINNIS
CLIO, S. C.
Age: 20   Degree: A.B.
Π Κ Φ

HELEN McKAY
ORANGEBURG, S. C.
Age: 19   Degree: A.B.
Woman's Association; Carolina Playmakers; Wigue
and Masque.
Π Β Φ

OLIVIA McKINNE
LOUISBURG, N. C.
Age: 19   Degree: A.B.
Treasurer Woman's Association
Π B Φ

WILLIAM MERRIMON McKINNEY, JR.
GREENSBORO, N. C.
Age: 20   Degree: B.S.

CALVIN STURGIS McLAUGHLIN
CHARLOTTE, N. C.
Age: 20   Degree: A.B.
Di Senate.
Σ E

JAMES LYTCH McNAIR, JR.
LAURINBURG, N. C.
Age: 20   Degree: B.S. Commerce
Π K A

ARTHUR DENNIS McNEILL
FAIR BLUFF, N. C.
Age: 25   Degree: Ph.G.

EDWARD ALEXANDER McNEILL
JEFFERSON, N. C.
Age: 21   Degree: A.B.

GARLAND McPHERSON
HIGH POINT, N. C.
Age: 20   Degree: A.B.
Tar Heel Staff, (2); Y.M.C.A. Cabinet; Treasurer
Di Senate, (3); President Di Senate, (4); Business
Manager Carolina Magazine, (2); Business Manager
Carolina Buccaneer, (3); Commencement Debater.
Σ Δ

ANGUS RAYMOND McRACHEN
SHANNON, N. C.
Age: 25   Degree: A.B. Education

JAMES EDWARD MAGNER

PHILADELPHIA, PA.

Age: 25   Degree: LL.B.

Athletic Council; Monogram Club; Executive Committee Monogram Club; Varsity Football, (2, 3, 4); Varsity Baseball. (2, 3, 4).

Σ Φ E, Φ A Δ

ROBERT DEWEY MARSHALL

GRANITE FALLS, N. C.

Age: 25   Degree: A.B. Education

Di Senate.

CLARENCE HERBERT MASON

NEWPORT, N. C.

Age: 23   Degree: A.B. Education

GLENWOOD CROWDER MEADS

WEEKSVILLE, N. C.

Age: 24   Degree: LL.B.

Δ Θ Φ

JOHN MEBANE

GREENSBORO, N. C.

Age: 20   Degree: A.B.

Associate Editor Carolina Magazine, (3); Editor
Carolina Magazine; Managing Editor Tar Heel, (2);
Associate Editor Daily Tar Heel; Managing Editor
Carolina Buccaneer, (3); Amphoterothen; Carolina
Tulane Varsity Debate.

Σ Δ

ANNE CAMBRELENG MELICK

ELIZABETH CITY, N. C.

Age: 20   Degree: A.B. Education

Playmakers; Vice-President Woman's Association.

Π Β Φ

EDWARD EMERSON MENDENHALL, JR.

GREENSBORO, N. C.

Age: 20   Degree: B.S. Commerce

Δ Σ Φ

ALBERT LEWIS MERCER

BEULAVILLE, N. C.

Age: 23   Degree: A.B. Education

GRADY MERCER
BEULAVILLE, N. C.
Age: 22   Degree: A.B. Education

ROBERT CHARLES MERRITT, JR.
WILMINGTON, N. C.
Age: 22   Degree: B.S. Commerce
Inter-fraternity Council.
Δ Σ Φ, Α Κ Ψ

WILLIAM EDGAR MERRITT
CHAPEL HILL, N. C.
Age: 20   Degree: A.B. Education
Freshman Friendship Council; Tennis Team, (2, 3, 4); Captain Tennis Team. (4).

JOHN MOSES MEWBORN
SNOW HILL, N. C.
Age: 23   Degree: B.S. Medicine
Freshman Inter-collegiate Debate; Phi Assembly; Speaker Pro-Tem. (3); Varsity Wrestling, (2, 3); Y.M.C.A. Cabinet, (2, 3); Varsity Debate, (2, 3); Whitehead Medical Society. (3, 4); Elisha Mitchell Scientific Society.
Τ Κ Α

YACKETY YACK

WESLEY LEE MONTGOMERY

BUNN, N. C.

Age: 22   Degree: A.B. Education

Wake Forest College; Y.M.C.A.; Debate Club;
Tar Heel Reporter; North Carolina Club.

JAMES ASHBY MOORE

SCOTLAND NECK, N. C.

Age: 25   Degree: B.S. Civil Engineering

American Society of Civil Engineers.

STEPHANIE MOORE

FAISON, N. C.

Age: 20   Degree: A.B.

WILLIAM BREWER MORGAN

PITTSBORO, N. C.

Age: 20   Degree: B.S. Commerce

Secretary Senior Class.

ROBERT LONG MURPHY
SALISBURY, N. C.

Age: 21   Degree: A.B.

Σ Ν, Φ Β Κ

RUTH NEWELL
SCOTLAND NECK, N. C.

Age: 23   Degree: A.B.

DAVID ANDERSON NIMS
MOUNT HOLLY, N. C.

Age: 22   Degree: B.S. Elec. Engineering

Vice-President Senior Class; Grail; Amphoterothen; Y.M.C.A. Cabinet; Varsity Track, (2, 3, 4); Captain Track, (4); Monogram Club; A. I. E. E.; Commencement Marshal; German Club; Cabin; Playmakers; Inter-fraternity Council.

Φ Κ Σ

FRANK CHURCH O'NEIL
HENDERSON, N. C.

Age: 22   Degree: A.B.

Freshman Friendship Council; Y.M.C.A. Cabinet; Elisha Mitchell Scientific Society.

Π Κ Φ

WALTER LESTUS OWEN

ROSEBORO, N. C.

Age: 21   Degree: B.S. Commerce

Σ Z

SAMUEL EUGENE PACE

LEAKSVILLE, N. C.

Age: 22   Degree: B.S. Medicine

Σ E, Δ Κ Κ, Φ Β Κ

JULIAN IVANHOE PALMORE

COLLEGE PARK, MD.

Age: 20   Degree: B.S. Civil Engineering

Minotaurs; Gorgon's Head; German Club; Vice-
President German Club; Assistant Leader Fall German; Freshman Tennis Team; German Club Executive Committee; A. S. C. E.

Σ Ν

B. MOORE PARKER

RALEIGH, N. C.

Age: 21   Degree: A.B.

Sub-Assistant Manager Basketball; Y. M. C. A. Cabinet; Di Senate; Tar Heel Staff, (1, 2, 3); Col-
lections Manager Tar Heel, (2); Assistant Business
Manager Tar Heel, (3); Inter-fraternity Council;
Executive Committee Junior Class; Business Manager Yackety-Yack, (4); Publications Union Board.

Σ Φ Ε, Ε Φ Δ

HARRY OLIVER PARKER
RALEIGH, N. C.
Age: 22   Degree: B.S. Commerce

JOHN WILLIAM PARKER
MURFREESBORO, N. C.
Age: 20   Degree: A.B. Education
Playmakers; Student Entertainment Committee.

WILLIAM CAREY PARKER
RALEIGH, N. C.
Age: 20   Degree: A.B.

ROBERT LEE PARLIER
KINGS CREEK, N. C.
Age: 26   Degree: A.B. Education
Cross Country Team.

PAUL RAYMOND PATTEN
NEW BERN N. C.

Age: 20   Degree: B.S. Commerce

Y.M.C.A. Cabinet; Glee Club, (1, 2, 3, 4); Band,
(3, 4); Manager Band, (4).

GRADON O'KELLY PENDERGRAFT
CHAPEL HILL, N. C.

Age: 25   Degree: B.S. Commerce

Circulation Manager Tar Heel, (3).

WILLIAM A. PERRY
CHAPEL HILL, N. C.

Age: 22   Degree: B.S. Chem. Engineering

Freshman Track; Varsity Track, (2, 3, 4); Monogram Club.

CARL LEE PETREE
WINSTON-SALEM, N. C.

Age: 23   Degree: B.S. Mech. Engineering

Boxing, (2, 3); American Society of Mechanical
Engineers.

Coy Tatum Phillips
WINSTON-SALEM, N. C.
Age: 25   Degree: A.B. Education
Debate Squad; Di Senate.

William Arthur Phillips
GRIFTON, N. C.
Age: 23   Degree: B.S. Commerce

John Baptist Pittana
UDINE, ITALY
Age: 27   Degree: B.S. Mech. Engineering
E Φ Δ

John Gerald Pleasant
ANGIER, N. C.
Age: 22   Degree: A.B. Education
Phi Assembly; North Carolina Club.

JAMES GREGORY POOLE
VIRGILINA, VA.
Age: 21   Degree: A.B.
Σ Δ

FRANCIS ROSS PORTER
MONROE, N. C.
Age: 21   Degree: B.S. Commerce

DOUGLAS LATEN POTTER
WEST PALM BEACH, FLA.
Age: 20   Degree: A.B.
Amphoterothen; Grail; Tennis Squad, (4).
Β Θ Π, Ε Φ Δ

JOHN C. QUICKEL
GASTONIA, N. C.
Age: 22   Degree: B.S. Medicine
Φ Χ

GEORGE RACE

CINCINNATI, OHIO

Age: 22   Degree: A.B.

Freshman Basketball Team; Vice-President Wigue and Masque; Minotaurs; German Club; President German Club, (4); Glee Club; Gimghouls; Pan-hellenic Council.

B Θ Π

RALPH L. RANDELL

JAMESTOWN, N. Y.

Age: 24   Degree: A.B.

Χ Φ

FRED C. RANKIN

BELMONT, N. C.

Age: 21   Degree: B.S. Civil Engineering

American Society of Civil Engineers.

Φ Κ Δ

LEONARD ERASTUS REAVES, JR.

RAEFORD, N. C.

Age: 21   Degree: Ph.G.

American Pharmaceutical Association; Freshman Tennis.

Σ Φ Ε, Κ Ψ

THOMAS BEATTY RECTOR

ASHEVILLE, N. C.

Age: 20   Degree: A.B.

Treasurer Senior Class; Di Senate; Clerk Di Senate,
(4); President Di Senate, (4).

Δ Θ Φ, Ε Φ Δ

JOHN CHARLES REDDING

TRINITY, N. C.

Age: 21   Degree: B.S.   Commerce

Δ Λ Τ, Δ Σ Π

CHARLES MAURICE REDFERN, JR.

MONROE, N. C.

Age: 21   Degree: A.B.

Minotaurs; Cabin; Y.M.C.A. Cabinet; German Club;
Football Squad, (2, 3, 4).

Σ Ν

RALPH CONNOR REID

CHARLOTTE, N. C.

Age: 22   Degree: A.B.   Education

Glee Club; Cheerios, (1, 2); Wrestling, (3); Nature
Study Club, (2).

BENJAMIN BROWNING ROACH

WHITEVILLE, N. C.

Age: 20   Degree: A.B. Journalism

Daily Tar Heel Staff, (3, 4); Assistant Sports Editor Tar Heel, (4); German Club; Glee Club; Yackety Yack; Cercle Francais; North Carolina Club; Buccaneer; Deutsche Verein.

ALFRED C. ROGERS

WARSAW, N. C.

Δge: 22   Degree: B.S. Commerce

CARL KING RUST

BRISTOL, VA.

Age: 22   Degree: A.B.

Acacia.

GEORGE W. SANDERS

MONTCLAIR, N. J.

Age: 21   Degree: A.B.

Freshman Wrestling Team; Varsity Wrestling, (2, 3, 4); Executive Committee German Club; Coop; Manager Coop; Sheiks; Gimghouls.

Σ A E

EARLIE C. SANDERSON
WALLACE, N. C.

Age: 21   Degree: A.B. Education

CLARENCE ODELL SAPP
WINSTON-SALEM, N. C.

Age: 24   Degree: LL.B.

Freshman Football; Varsity Football, (4, 5); Varsity Boxing, (4, 5); Varsity Baseball, (2); President Athletic Association; Monogram Club; Carolina Playmakers; Leader Junior Dance; Inter-fraternity Council; German Club; Assistant Coach Freshman Football and Baseball; Coach Freshman Boxing.
Σ Φ E, Φ A Δ

HERMAN WALKER SCHNELL
CHAPEL HILL, N. C.

Age: 20   Degree: A.B.

"13" Club; President "13" Club, (4); German Club; Assistant Manager Wrestling, (2); Manager Wrestling, (3); Manager Boxing, (4); Monogram Club.
Δ Ψ

JAMES PAUL SCURLOCK
GREENSBORO, N. C.

Age: 23   Degree: B.S. Civil Engineering

Wigue and Masque; A. S. C. E.; Glee Club, (1, 2, 3, 4); President Glee Club, (4); Track Squad, (1, 2); Football Squad, (1, 2).

Φ Σ K, Φ M A

CHARLES BION SEARS
WHITEVILLE, N. C.
Age: 19   Degree: Ph.G.

CHARLES JOHN SHANNON, IV
CAMDEN, S. C.
Age: 22   Degree: B.S. Commerce
Cabin; President of Cabin; Tar Heel Business Staff, (1).

Σ A E

JOHN CRAIG SHELTON
CHARLOTTE, N. C.
Age: 22   Degree: B.S. Commerce
Sub-Assistant Manager of Track, (1, 2); German Club; Wigue and Masque.

Σ X, A K Ψ

JAMES EMORY SHERWOOD
GREENSBORO, N. C.
Age: 22   Degree: B.S. Elec. Engineering
American Institute of Electrical Engineers.

WALES FRANKLIN SIGMON

ALEXIS, N. C.

Age: 24   Degree: A.B. Education

HOWARD HOLMES SIMPSON

ROSEBORO, N. C.

Age: 21   Degree: A.B. Education

Cross Country, (3).

MARCUS B. SIMPSON

UNIONVILLE, N. C.

Age: 21   Degree: A.B. Education

Dialectic Senate; Dormitory Council, (3); Sergeant at Arms in Dialectic Senate; Mary D. Wright Debate Committee.

GENE CECIL SIPE

CHERRYVILLE, N. C.

Age: 21   Degree: A.B. Education

ROBERT CECIL SISK

BRYSON CITY, N. C.

Age: 20   Degree: Pharmacy

American Pharmaceutical Association.

Φ Δ Χ

JACOB EDWARD SKINNER

GREENVILLE, N. C.

Age: 21   Degree: B.S. Elec. Engineering

American Institute of Electrical Engineering; Taylor Society.

CHARLES LEE SMITH

RALEIGH, N. C.

Age: 22   Degree: A.B.

Sheiks; Vice-President of Sheiks. (2); Commence-
ment Marshal, (3); Freshman Football and Track
Team; Varsity Football; Track Squad, (2, 3);
Woodberry Forest Club; German Clubs.

Z Ψ

JAMES KENNETH SMITH

DALLAS, TEXAS

Age: 22   Degree: B.S. Commerce.

Monogram Club.

Δ Σ Π

WILLIE BALLANCE SMITH
FREMONT, N. C.

Age: 24   Degree: A.B.

THOMAS MILLER SNYDER
SALISBURY, N. C.

Age: 21   Degree: A.B.

Δ T Δ

LEON A. SPAULDING
ATKINS, PA.

Age: 21   Degree: A.B.
Football, (2, 3, 4).

Σ A E

WILLIAM WESLEY SPEIGHT
SPRINGHOPE, N. C.

Age: 21   Degree: B.S. Commerce

Debate Council; Speaker of Phi Assembly; Tar Heel
Staff, (2, 4); Inter-collegiate Debates; Carolina vs.
Virginia, Radio Debate; Carolina vs., Marquette Uni-
versity Debate; Carolina vs. Emory.

Δ Θ Φ, T K A

SAMUEL EDWARD SPITZER
YONKERS, N. Y.
Age: 21   Degree: A.B.

ROBERT EDWARD STANTON
ELIZABETH CITY, N. C.
Age: 21   Degree: A.B.

FRANK PHILIPS STIMSON
STATESVILLE, N. C.
Age: 23 Degree: B.S. Commerce
Glee Club, (2, 3, 4).
Σ Z

GEORGE PRYOR STONE, JR.
GREENSBORO, N. C.
Age: 23 Degree: B.S. Commerce

LEON GIRLEY STONE
GREENSBORO, N. C.
Age: 21   Degree: B.S. Commerce

ARTHUR THOMAS STRICKLAND, JR.
WILSON, N. C.
Age: 21   Degree: B.S. Medicine
Λ Κ Κ

JACOB HILL STRONG
RHINEBECK, NEW YORK
Age: 20   Degree: A.B.
Φ Γ Δ

MILTON STANLEY STURM
ATLANTA, GA.
Age: 21   Degree: B.S. Commerce
Δ Σ Φ

MALCOLM GREER STUTZ
SOUTHERN PINES, N. C.
Age: 20   Degree: A.B.
Λ X Λ

GRANVILLE HAMILTON SWOPE
BALTIMORE, MD.
Age: 21   Degree: A.B.
X Ψ

EDWARD FORT TAYLOR
OXFORD, N. C.
Age: 23   Degree: LL.B.
Inter-fraternity Council; Member of North Caro-
lina Bar.
Θ K N

HAROLD HENRY TEITELBAUM
JERSEY CITY, N. J.
Age: 21   Degree: B.S. Medicine

AMOS LEE THOMAS
MARSHVILLE, N. C.
Age: 20   Degree: A.B. Education

PHILLIP LANGSTON THOMAS
ERWIN, N. C.
Age: 23   Degree: Ph.G.
Φ Δ Θ, Κ Ψ

LOY DURANT THOMPSON, JR.
GREENSBORO, N. C.
Age: 21   Degree: A.B.
Summer School Student Council '29; Manager Var-
sity Baseball, (4); Monogram Club; German Club.
Σ Χ

FRANCIS ROGERS TOMS
PETERSBURG, VA.
Age: 21   Degree: B.S. Elec. Engineering
Coop; Minotaurs; Gimghouls; A. I. E. E.
Κ Σ, Τ Β Π, Φ Ζ Ν, Φ Β Κ

MARGARET LOUISE TROUTMAN
STATESVILLE, N. C.
Age: 19   Degree: A.B.

FRANK KENYON TURNER
HILLSBORO, N. C.
Age: 21   Degree: A.B. Education
Band; Philanthropic Society; Boxing Team.

LAWRENCE EVERETT TULLOCH
DANVILLE, VA.
Age: 21   Degree: B.S. Elec. Engineering

OSCAR LOGAN UMSTEAD
STEM, N. C.
Age: 22   Degree: Ph.G.
Κ Ψ

WINGATE EGERTON UNDERHILL

LOUISBURG, N. C.

Age: 21   Degree: C.E.

American Society of Civil Engineers; German Club.

Σ N, T B Π, Φ B K

THADDEUS GILBERT UPCHURCH

APEX, N. C.

Age: 20   Degree: B.S. Medicine

Vice-President of Medical Society; Elisha Mitchell Scientific Society.

Θ K Ψ

HAROLD E. URIST

FLUSHING, N. Y.

Age: 21   Degree: A.B.

FRANCIS DU-BOSE UZZELL

CHAPEL HILL, N. C.

Age: 21   Degree: A.B.

Freshman Friendship Council; Sophomore Y.M.C.A. Cabinet; Junior-Senior Y.M.C.A. Cabinet; Phi Assembly, (1, 2, 3, 4); Freshman Cross Country; Freshman Track; Varsity Cross Country, (2); Tar Heel Staff, (2).

RAYMOND DAVIS VOGLER

MOUNT AIRY, N. C.

Age: 20   Degree: A.B. Education

CHARLES EDWARD WADDELL, JR.

BILTMORE, N. C.

Age: 22   Degree: Civil Engineering

Tennis Team, (2, 3, 4); Captain Tennis Team, (3); Sheiks; Gimghouls; William Cain Society, (2, 3, 4); President of William Cain Society, (4); Golden Fleece.

Β Θ Π, Τ Β Π, Φ Β Κ

EDMUND LAW WADDILL

HENDERSON, N. C.

Age: 20   Degree: B.S. Commerce

Cabin; "13" Club.

Δ Τ Δ, Δ Κ Ψ

RICHARD MONTAGU WALFORD, JR.

SHREVEPORT, LA.

Age: 22   Degree: B.S. Civil Engineering

American Society of Civil Engineers; German Club.

Σ Φ Σ

THOMAS ROGER WALKER
GREENSBORO, N. C.
Age: 21   Degree: B.S. Commerce
Λ Χ Α

HERBERT CHRISTY WALL
SOPHIA, N. C.
Age: 20   Degree: A.B.
Φ Β Κ

DAVID JACKSON WARD
WELDON, N. C.
Age: 21   Degree: A.B.
Κ Α

DEAN A. WARD
ZIRCONIA, N. C.
Age: 25   Degree: A.B. Education

JOSEPH TYSON WARD
CHAPEL HILL, N. C.
Age: 18   Degree: A.B. Education

NEEDHAM EDGAR WARD
CHAPEL HILL, N. C.
Age: 20   Degree: B.S. Medicine
Φ X

JOHN WALLER WARDLAW
PLAINFIELD, N. J.
Age: 23   Degree: B.S. Commerce; LL.B.
Jack Wardlaw and his Orchestra; Organizer of the
Carolina Banjo Boys; German Club; Di Senate;
Wardlaw School Alumni Association.
Φ K Σ

ROBERT HOKE WEBB
RALEIGH, N. C.
Age: 21   Degree: A.B.
Freshman Boxing Team; Varsity Boxing Team;
Cabin.
Σ A E, Φ B K

JAMES WILLIAM WEBSTER
LEAKSVILLE, N. C.
Age: 19   Degree: A.B.

EUGENE ERNEST WELLS
GREENVILLE, S. C.
Age: 21   Degree: B.S. Commerce
Sheiks; Coop; Secretary Coop, (3); President
Coop. (4).

K Δ

JOHN ROBERT WELLS
MURPHY, N. C.
Age: 21   Degree: A.B. Education
Θ Φ

KATHARINE PLATT WELLS
LAUREL, MISS.
Age: 20   Degree: A.B.
President of Woman's Association.

CHARLES HARDEN WEST
GREENSBORO, N. C.
Age: 22   Degree: B.S. Civil Engineering

JOSEPH ROBERT WESTMORELAND
CANTON, N. C.
Age: 22   Degree: B.S. Medicine
Baseball, (1, 2, 3, 4); Captain of Baseball, (4);
Monogram Club.

A K K

WILLIS GUILFORD WHICHARD
GREENVILLE, N. C.
Age: 21   Degree: A.B.
Pitt County Club; Vice-President Pitt County Club,
(1); Secretary-Treasurer Pitt County Club, (2);
Track Squad, (1); Business Manager Carolina Re-
porter.

Σ Z

RICHARD HARPER WHITAKER
OAK RIDGE, N. C.
Age: 22   Degree: A.B.

WILLIAM BURTON WHITE

TOWNSVILLE, N. C.

Age: 21   Degree: B.S. Elec. Engineering

A. I. E. E.; Treasurer A. I. E. E., (4).

Θ Φ, Φ Z N, T B Π

JAMES LUCIUS WHITLEY

ENFIELD, N. C.

Age: 23   Degree: B.S. Commerce

GUYON EUGENE WHITTEN

MARION, N. C.

Age: 20   Degree: B.S. Commerce

GEORGE WILCOX

NEWPORT, N. C.

Age: 23   Degree: A.B. Education

CHARLES FREDRICK WILLIAMS
RALEIGH, N. C.

Age: 22   Degree: A.B.

Freshman Football; Freshman Track; Basketball
Squad, (1, 2, 4).

Z Ψ

JOSEPH CARLYLE WILLIAMS
LINDEN, N. C.

Age: 20   Degree: A.B. Education

Pres. Di Senate; Pres. Debate Council; Senior Class
Ex. Com.; Asst. Ed. and Columnist of the Tar
Heel; Book Ed. Carolina Magazine; Yackety Yack
Staff; Buccaneer Staff; Winner Bingham Memorial
Medal; Winner Mary D. Wright Memorial Medal;
Freshman Intercollegiate Debater; Varsity Intercol-
legiate Debater; Pres. Debate Squad.

Δ Θ Φ, Ε Φ Δ, Φ Κ Δ, Τ Κ Α

LENA MAE WILLIAMS
CHAPEL HILL, N. C.

Age: 20   Degree: A.B.

COLIE VERNON WILLIAMSON
HOBUCKEN, N. C.

Age: 21   Degree: A.B.

Student Council.

BONNY COLUMBUS WILSON

GLENVILLE, N. C.

Age: 25   Degree: A.B. Education

Tar Heel Staff, (1, 2); Y.M.C.A. Cabinet, (1, 2, 3); Playmakers, (2, 3, 4); Di Senate; Vice-President Di Senate, (3); Freshman, Sophomore, and Junior De bates; Winner Mangum Medal, (3); Debate Council, (3); Yackety Yack Staff, (2, 3); Carolina Magazine Staff, (3); Glee Club, (3); Manager of Boxing Team, (3).

X T

JANET H. WILSON

MORRISTOWN, N. J.

Age: 20   Degree: A.B.

FRANK WILSON, JR.

GREENVILLE, N. C.

Age: 20   Degree: B.S. Medicine

German Club; Band, (1, 2, 3); Executive Committee Senior Class; Medical Society; Elisha Mitchell Scientific Society.

Θ K Ψ

JOHN FLEMING WILY, JR.

DURHAM, N. C.

Age: 23   Degree: A.B.

German Club; Treasurer Sophomore Class; Sheiks; Coop; Varsity Basketball Squad; Senior Order of Daviens; Gimghouls; Chairman Executive Committee Senior Class; Leader Gimghoul Dance.

Σ Δ E

GEORGE CALDWELL WINECOFF, JR.

GASTONIA, N. C.

Age: 20   Degree: B.S. Commerce

Tennis Squad.

Δ Σ Π

MARSHALL FRANKLIN WOODALL

BENSON, N. C.

Age: 20   Degree: B.S. Commerce

ERWIN CARLYLE WOODARD

PRINCETON, N. C.

Age: 20   Degree: A.B. Education

WILLIAM THOMAS WOODARD

KENLY, N. C.

Age: 22   Degree: B.S. Commerce

ROBIN NATHANIEL WOOTEN

HARMONY, N. C.

Age: 21   Degree: A.B. Education

CREIGHTON WRENN

GARNER, N. C.

Age: 22   Degree: A.B.

Monogram Club.

SHERMAN A. YEARGAN

GARNER, N. C.

Age: 20   Degree: B.S. Commerce

JOHN OTIS YOUNGBLOOD

FLETCHER, N. C.

Age: 20   Degree: A.B. Education

FRANCIS VINCENT ZAPPA

BALTIMORE, MD.

Age: 24   Degree: A.B.

E Φ Δ

ROBERT LYLES ZEALY

GOLDSBORO, N. C.

Age: 20   Degree: A.B.

Grail; Wrestling Team; Executive Committee German Club.

Z Ψ, Φ B K, E Φ Δ

HENRY HERMANN ZURBURG

ASHEVILLE, N. C.

Δge: 22   Degree: A.B.

SAMUEL RICHARDSON WILEY

GREENSBORO, N. C.

Age: 20   Degree: B.S. Commerce

Taylor Society; Pres. Rifle Club.

Σ Δ, Δ Σ Π

MARION ALEXANDER
Best Business Man

J. C. WILLIAMS
Best Writer

CHARLES
WADDELL

*Best
All Round*

RED GREENE
Chief Politician

ARCHIE ALLEN
Most Social

PHOEBE
HARDING

*Most
Dramatic*

BEATTY RECTOR
*Biggest Bull
Shooter*

FLEMING WILY
Most Influential

FENTON ADKINS
Sweetest & Most Popular

PAUL CARR
Best Speaker

TOM HUNTER
Most Retiring

DAVID NIMS
Best Natured

HARRY GALLAND
Most Original

[110]

Weakening

JUNIORS

HUDSON

MARPET

WEEKS

DAVIS

FUSSELL

Officers of the Junior Class

JAMES SPEARMAN HUDSON _____ President

ARTHUR ROBERT MARPET_____ Vice-President

CLARENCE JOHNSON WEEKS _____ Secretary

OBIE GUSS DAVIS _____ Treasurer

LUCIAN H. FUSSELL _____ Representative on Student Council

FRANK M. ADAMS
Dillon, S. C.
Θ Κ Ν

B. D. ARNOLD
Fuquay Springs,
N. C.

Freshman Track; Varsity
Track.

THURSTON RAY
ADAMS
LaGrange, N. C.
Η Κ Φ

JOHN B. ASHCRAFT
Monroe, N. C.
Π Κ Α

R. M. ALBRIGHT
Raleigh, N. C.

Assistant Editor Yackety
Yack; Speaker Phi As-
sembly; Varsity Wres-
tling; Debate Council;
Inter-fraternity Council;
Junior Class Executive
Committee; Secretary
Freshman Friendship
Council; Y. M. C. A.
Cabinet; German Club
Executive Committee;
Grail; Amphoterothen;
Sheiks.
Ζ Ψ, Τ Κ Α

CALLIS H. ATKINS
White Plains, N. C.
Θ Φ

A. L. ALEXANDER
Statesville, N. C.
Α Χ Σ

GEORGE L. BAGBY
Charlotte, N. C.

Minotaurs; Gimghouls;
Freshman Track; Varsity
Track; Monogram Club;
Inter-fraternity Council;
Coop; German Club;
Leader Sophomore Hop.

Κ Σ

ROBERT L. ALPHIN
Wendell, N. C.

MERRITT C. BAKER
Buffalo, N. Y.
Θ Κ Ν

[113]

OTIS W. BAKER
Carthage, N. C.

LEXIE G. BAREFOOT
Four Oaks, N. C.

K Ψ

T. R. BALDWIN
Randleman, N. C.

S. A. BARRETT
Fayetteville, N. C.

J. M. BALEY, JR.
Asheville, N. C.

Debate Team

C. R. BAUCOM
Marshville, N. C.

Freshman Cross Country;
Varsity Cross Country;
Freshman Track; Varsity
Track; Monogram Club.

C. H. BALLARD, JR.
Kinston, N. C.

Phi Assembly; Rifle
Club.

JOHN C. BEAKLEY
Asheville, N. C.

R. N. BARBER
Waynesville, N. C.

Π K A, Δ Σ Π

CLAY C. BELL
Rockingham, N. C.

KENNETH A. BELL
New Bern, N. C.

Freshman Football;
Freshman Basketball;
Varsity Football Squad;
Varsity Track Squad;
German Club; Y. M. C.
A. Cabinet.

Θ Χ

JOHN S. BIVENS
Monroe, N. C.

MRS. P. B. BENNETT
Chapel Hill, N. C.

SADIE M. BIVENS
Monroe, N. C.

G. R. BENTON
Fremont, N. C.

Φ Δ Θ

THOMAS J. BIVENS
Monroe, N. C.

ROBERT E. BETTS
Macon, N. C.

Buccaneer Editorial
Staff.

STANLEY R. BLAIR
Trinity, N. C.

W. A. BIGGS, JR.
Rockingham, N. C.

WILLIAM K. BLAIR
Greensboro, N. C.

Χ Ψ

B. L. BOYETTE
Murfreesboro,
N. C.

J. L. BROWN, JR.
Concord, N. C.

K Σ

J. T. BOYSWORTH
Norwood, N. C.

RUFUS A. BROWN
Concord, N. C.

Band.

K Σ

F. M. BRICKMAN
Georgetown, S. C.

Buccaneer; Wigue and
Masque; Cabin.

Φ K Σ

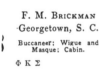

H. T. BROWNE
Nashville, Tenn.

Amphoterothen.

B Θ Π

A. M. BROWN
Franklin, Pa.

Ψ Υ

T. H. BRASWELL
Castalia. N. C.

Φ Δ X

EUGENE F. BROWN
Hillsboro, N. C.

N. L. BRYAN, JR.
Winter Park, Fla.

William Cain American
Society Civil Engineers;
Freshman Tennis; Varsity
Tennis.

Σ Z

RUBY D. BUCK
Bald Mountain,
N. C.

X Ω

W. L. CARLISLE
Bennettsville, S. C.

Σ X, A K Ψ

CECIL F. BULLARD
Fayetteville, N. C.

Freshman Track; Varsity
Track.

JOE A. CARPENTER
Gastonia, N. C.

German Club.

Σ Φ Σ

FRED B. BUNCH
Statesville, N. C.

Y. M. C. A. Cabinet;
Di Senate; Sub-Assistant
Basketball Manager.

Σ Z

DANIEL W. CARTER
Pitman, N. J.

WILLIAM L. BURKE
Burlington, N. C.

MARY A. CARTER
Fayetteville, Tenn.

X Ω

JAMES ADAM BURT
Biscoe, N. C.

Freshman Baseball;
Varsity Baseball.

T. J. CHACONAS
Washington, D. C.

C. G. CHATHAM
Elkin, N. C.

Golf Team; Manager
Golf Team; Inter-frater-
nity Council; Minotaurs;
German Club.

Δ K E

B. F. COFFIELD
Columbia, N. C.

PAGE CHOATE
Salisbury, N. C.

MILTON COHEN
Fushing, N. Y.

Tar Heel Business Staff;
Inter-fraternity Council.

Φ A

H. F. CHRISCO
Badin, N. C.

University Band.

A Λ T

JAMES L. COLEY
Wilmington, N. C.

Σ Z

T. M. CLELAND
New York, N. Y.

Φ Δ Θ

C. W. CONSTANTINE
Birmingham, Ala.

Assistant Manager Bas-
ketball; Cabin; German
Club.

Σ A E

C. L. CLODFELTER
Thomasville, N. C.

Φ Δ X

WILLIAMS COOPER
Oxford, N. C.

Z Ψ

G. T. CORNWELL
Lawndale, N. C.

Cleveland County Club;
Y. M. C. A. Quartette;
Wrestling Squad.

FRANK L. CRANE
Waxhaw, N. C.

Varsity Cross Country;
Freshman Basketball;
Freshman Track.

JACK B. COURSEY
Southern Pines,
N. C.

Glee Club.

X Φ

W. S. CRAWFORD
Mebane, N. C.

MARION R. COWPER
Kinston, N. C.

American Society of Civil
Engineers; Varsity Foot-
ball; Varsity Wrestling;
Freshman Wrestling;
Monogram Club; Assist-
ant Leader Junior Prom;
German Club.

Z Ψ

B. L. CREDLE
Swan Quarter, N.C

ELSA S. CRAIG
Chapel Hill, N. C.

S. ELLIS CREW
Pleasant Hill,
N. C.

Φ Γ Δ

RAY P. CRAIG
Stanley, N. C.

Φ Δ X

JOHN H. CROOM
Fayetteville, N. C.

Σ Δ

C. F. CRUTCHFIELD
North Wilkesboro,
N. C.

Wilkes County Club.

Λ Λ T

WALTER A. DALEY
Orlando, Fla

Inter-fraternity Council;
Cabin.

Φ Δ Θ

W. H. CULBRETH
Raeford, N. C.

Freshman Football.

E. P. DAMERON
Clinton, N. C.

Varsity Basketball;
Varsity Track; Mono-
gram Club.

Σ N

IDA W. CURRIE
Clarkton, N. C.

X Ω

H. L. DANIEL
Clearwater, Fla.

X Ω

JOHN A. CURRIE
New York, N. Y.

CLARENCE DAVIS
Waxhaw, N. C.

JAY L. CURTIS
Patterson, N. C.

Associate Editor Caro-
lina Magazine.

Σ Δ

JEFFERSON DAVIS
Waxhaw, N. C.

OBIE GUSS DAVIS
Omaha, Texas

Treasurer Junior Class;
Varsity Boxing.

Σ Z

D. C. DeWOLFE, JR.
Monroe, Conn.

Φ Δ Θ

RALPH W. DAVIS
Harmony, N. C.

WILLIAM G. DIKE
Philadelphia, Pa.

Σ Φ Σ

W. F. DAY, JR.
Greenwich, Conn.

Wesleyan, (1, 2); As-
sistant Stage Manager
Playmakers.

X Ψ

GLENN S. DICKSON
Helton, N. C.

Dialectic Senate; Deut-
sche Verein.

H. M. DELLINGER
Stanley, N. C.

Φ Δ X

N. W. DOCKERY
Rockingham, N. C.

Photograph Editor Yack-
ety Yack; Y. M. C. A.
Cabinet; Freshman Box-
ing; Dialectic Senate;
Chemistry Club; Blue
Key Society; German
Club.

Σ X

ROBERT F. DEWEY
Chicago, Ill.

Φ Γ Δ

GAVIN DORTCH, JR.
Raleigh, N. C.

Varsity Football; Sheiks;
Cimghoul.

Δ K E

J. W. Doughtie
Columbus, Ga.

Δ T Δ

Clyde M. Duncan
Beaufort, N. C.

Π Β Φ

T. B. Douglas
High Point, N. C.

Alembric Club; Mathe-
matics Club; Holt
Scholarship.

W. Dunn, Jr.
New Bern, N. C.

Business Staff Yackety
Yack; Assistant Manager
Track; Minotaurs;
Gimghoul.

Δ Κ Ε

Virginia Douglas
Greensboro, N. C.

W. Clyde Dunn
Kinston, N. C.

Assistant Editor Yacketv
Yack; Tar Heel Staff;
President Publication
Union Board; President
Sophomore Y. M. C. A.
Cabinet; Treasurer
Freshman Class; Junior
Class Executive Com-
mittee; Dialectic Senate;
Taylor Society; Coop;
German Club.

Κ Σ, Ε Φ Δ

Inez S. Dudley
Lake Landing,
N. C.

Joe C. Eagles
Wilson, N. C.

Sub-Assistant Manager
Basketball; Tar Heel
Staff, (1, 2, 3); Sports
Editor, (3); Y. M. C.
A., (1, 2, 3); Secretary,
(3); Sheiks; Ampho-
terothen; Grail; Cabin;
German Club.

Κ Σ

Charles C. Duffy
New Bern, N. C.

Phi Assembly; Glee
Club; German Club.

Δ Σ Φ

David C. Edwards
Walkertown, N. C.

Φ Κ Δ

C. P. ERICKSON
Oak Park, Ill.

Varsity Football, (2, 3);
Track, (3); A. S. C. E.;
Secretary, (2); Vice-
President, (3); Monogram
Club; Inter-fraternity
Council.

Δ T Ω

JAMES L. FEREBEE
West Allis, Wis.

Δ T Δ

WILLIAM E. EVANS
High Point, N. C.

FRED J. FERGUSON
Waynesville, N. C.

Y. M. C. A. Cabinet;
Monogram Club; Wres-
tling.

Δ Σ Π

C. H. FARRELL
Dunn, N. C.

Playmakers, (1, 2);
Yackety Yack Staff; Ad-
vertising Manager, (2);
Assistant Business Man-
ager, (3); Associate Ed-
itor Buccaneer; Assistant
Manager Boxing; Com-
mencement Marshal; Y.
M. C. A. Cabinet, (2,
3); German Club.

X Φ

ADAM FISHER, JR.
Charlotte, N. C.

Δ Ψ

ROBERT FARRELL
Aberdeen, N. C.

X Φ, Δ K Ψ

CARL H. FISHER
Salisbury, N. C.

Freshman Cross Coun-
try; Freshman Track;
Freshman Friendship
Council; Y. M. C. A.
Cabinet, (2, 3).

Δ Δ T

ELZADA FEASTER
Miami, Fla.

Playmakers.

Π B Φ

JAMES B. FISHER
Pittsburgh, Pa.

University of Pittsburgh,
(1).

ROSCOE B. FISHER
Salisbury, N. C.

Α Λ Τ, Τ Κ Α

ELLIS D. FYSAL
Wilson, N. C.

Freshman Football;
Freshman Baseball;
Varsity Football.

CHARLES E. FORD
Louisburg, N. C.

Minotaurs; Coop;
German Club.

Κ Σ

JOHN W. GARNER
Goldston, N. C.

BERRY G. FRENCH
Lumberton, N. C.

Φ Γ Δ

R. H. GARRETT
Washington, D. C.

Track Team; Monogram
Club.

Κ Α

NAHUM FRIEDMAN
Brooklyn, N. Y.

E. L. GASKILL
Sea Level, N. C.

LUCIAN H. FUSSELL
Rose Hill, N. C.

Student Council.

Φ Κ Δ

KENNETH A. GAY
Lawrence, Mass

Varsity Track Team.

Δ Ψ

PAUL L. GILBERT
Statesville, N. C.
A. S. C. E.; German
Club.
A T Ω

P. W. GLIDEWELL
Reidsville, N. C.
B Θ Π

M. P. GILMOUR, III
Wilmington, N. C.
German Club.
Σ A E

C. W. GOLDSTON
Goldston, N. C.

H. W. GLASCOCK
Raleigh, N. C.
X Ψ

MARJORIE GOOD
Columbia, S. C.

SAMUEL GLASS
Brooklyn, N. Y.
Φ A

JOHN F. GOODE
Woodard, N. C.

C. S. GLICKMAN
Brooklyn, N. Y.

J. B. GOODMAN
Altamont, N. C.

NOAH GOODRIDGE
New York, N. Y.

Freshman Friendship
Council; Freshman Box-
ing Team; Varsity Box-
ing Team; Monogram
Club; Cabin; Executive
Committee Junior Class.

Σ A E

J. C. GRAINGER
Wilmington, N. C.

Phi Assembly; Yackety
Yack, (2); "13" Club;
Cabin.

Δ Ψ

JAMES C. GOODWIN
Clifton Forge, Va.

Θ X

Elizabeth Grant
Wilmington, N. C.

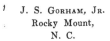

J. S. GORHAM, JR.
Rocky Mount,
N. C.

Freshman Friendship
Council; Y. M. C. A.
Cabinet, (2, 3); Treas-
urer Sophomore Cabinet;
Sub-Assistant Manager
Track; Phi Assembly.

A. T. GRIFFIN
Pine Tops, N. C.

J. M. GRAHAM
Baltimore, Md.

Δ Τ

J. O. GRIFFIN
Chapel Hill, N. C.

KATE C. GRAHAM
Durham, N. C.

Π B Φ

H. F. GRINDSTAFF
Sylvia, N. C.

ERNEST T. GROSS
Burlington, N. C.
A. I. E. E.; Rifle Club.
Θ Φ

L. T. HAMMOND
Asheboro, N. C.
Orchestra; Yackety Yack Staff; Di Senate; Glee Club.
Σ Φ E, E Φ Δ

J. W. GROTYOHANN
Brooklyn, N. Y.
Playmakers

J. M. HARRINGTON
Freeport, N. Y.
Ψ Τ

JUNE U. GUNTER
Sanford, N. C.
Di Senate; Yackety Yack Staff; Tar Heel Staff.
Σ Φ E

HENRY D. HARRIS
Durham, N. C.
Δ Σ Π

W. H. HADLEY, JR.
Siler City, N. C.

JAMES C. HARRIS
Inez, N. C.
Phi Assembly, (1, 2, 3); Reading Clerk Phi Assembly, (2); Treas. Phi Assembly, (3); Freshman Friendship Council; Y. M. C. A. Cabinet, (2, 3); Debate Squad, (1, 2, 3); Freshman Debate; Sophomore-Junior Intersociety Debate; Carolina-Marquette Debate; Mary D. Wright Debate; Debate Council, (3); Cross Country Squad, (2, 3); Tar Heel Business Staff, (2, 3); Collection Manager Tar Heel; Collection Manager Buccaneer; Gold Monogram.

EDWARD R. HAMER
McColl, S. C.
Y. M. C. A. Cabinet; Treasurer Y. M. C. A. Cabinet, (3); Buccaneer Business Staff; Yackety Yack Staff; Sub-Assistant Manager Basketball; Track Squad; Grail; Minotaurs; Cabin; Di Senate; Executive Committee Junior Class; Commencement Marshal; German Club.
Σ N, E Φ Δ

T K Λ

CLYDE L. HAWKINS
Bessemer City, N. C.
Di Senate.

C. P. Hayes, Jr.
Asheville, N. C.

American Institute of
Electrical Engineering.

Θ Φ

P. L. Henderson
Jersey City, N. C.

Playmakers.

Κ Σ

E. L. Haywood
Durham, N. C.

"13" Club; Yackety Yack
Staff, (3); Phi Assem-
bly, (1, 2, 3); Executive
Committee Phi Assem-
bly, (3); Assistant Man-
ager of Varsity Baseball;
Inter-collegiate Debate;
German Club; Leader
Fall German; Inter-
fraternity Council.

Χ Φ, Τ Κ Α

W. I. Henderson
Charlotte, N. C.

Y. M. C. A. Cabinets;
Coop; "13" Club; Di
Senate; Golf Squad;
Leader Junior Prom;
German Club.

Σ Ν, Α Κ Ψ

W. F. Haywood
Candor, N. C.

Charles H. Henry
Plainfield, N. J.

Assistant Cheer Leader.

Θ Κ Ν

H. Hechenbleikner
Charlotte, N. C.

M. George Henry
Chapel Hill, N. C.

Y. M. C. A. Cabinet.

Σ Δ

J. E. Heller
Brooklyn, N. Y.

Freshman Football; Var-
sity Football; Varsity
Wrestling; Ata Romani
Club.

C. A. Hensley, Jr.
Morganton, N. C.

A. I. E. E.; Rifle Club.

Θ Φ

JOSEPH F. HESTER
Washington, D. C.
Δ Σ Φ

GILES F. HORNEY
Greensboro, N. C.
A. I. E. E.

JOSEPHINE HILL
Burlington, N. C.
Π B Φ

M. A. HOUGHTON
Clayton, N. C.
Wrestling Squad.

EUGENE G. HINES
Goldsboro, N. C.
Σ N, A K Ψ

F. J. HOUSEHOLDER
Durham, N. C.
Λ X A, Φ M A

ELMER G. HOEFER
Chapel Hill, N. C.
- A. I. E. E.
Φ K Σ

R. E. HUBBARD
Clinton, N. C.
Cabin; German Club.
Φ Γ Δ

R. E. L. HOLT, JR.
Burlington, N. C.
Π K A

JAMES S. HUDSON
Dallas, Tex.
Captain Freshman Football; Varsity Football; "13" Club; Coop; President Junior Class; Monogram Club.

Σ A E

CLYDE E. HULON
Laurinburg, N. C.

F. W. JACKSON
Apex, N. C.

W. C. HUNSUCKER
Gibson, N. C.

HENRY T. JACKSON
Mount Olive, N. C.

FRED S. HUNTER
Huntersville, N. C.

LILLIE W. JACKSON
Eustis, Fla.

Π Β Φ

M. N. HUNTER
Huntersville, N. C.

F. G. JACOCKS, JR.
Elizabeth City,
N. C.

Band; Symphony Orchestra; German Club.

Σ Χ

JOHN D. IDOL
High Point, N. C.

Glee Club; Y. M. C. A. Cabinet; Buccaneer Staff; Grail.

J. S. JEMISON, JR.
Birmingham, Ala.

Business Staff Tar Heel.

Σ Α Ε

ESTHER JOHNSON
Milwaukee, N. C.

HERBERT W. JONES
Greensboro, N. C.

Inter-fraternity Council;
Band; Freshman Friend-
ship Council.

Φ Σ K, Φ M A

J. C. JOHNSON
Morven, N. C.

JOE PIPER JONES
Berryville, Va.

Grail; Amphoterothen. |

Σ Υ

J. J. JOHNSON
Siler, City, N. C.
Baseball Squad.

WILLIAM F. JONES
Charlotte, N. C.

Glee Club.

J. D. JOHNSON
Siler City, N. C.

T. R. KARRIKER
Mooresville, N. C.

Y. M. C. A. Cabinet;
Clerk Di Senate; Col-
lection Manager Tar
Heel.

Σ Φ E

P. G. JOHNSON, JR.
Asheville, N. C.

A. I. E. E.; Di Senate.

A. D. KINCAID, JR.
Charlotte, N. C.

Freshman Track Team;
Varsity Track Squad;
Yackety Yack Staff; Y.
M. C. A. Cabinet;
German Club.

Δ K E

A. M. KIRKPATRICK
Caldwell, N. J.
Φ Κ Σ

P. P. KJELLESVIG
Havana, Cuba
Secretary Spanish Club.
Δ Σ Φ, Ε Φ Δ

J. J. KIRKPATRICK
Caldwell, N. J.
Secretary Wigue and
Masque; Advertising
Manager Playmakers;
Glee Club.
Φ Κ _

GEORGE M. KOEHL
College Point, N.Y.
Δ Σ Φ

LEONARD B. KISER
Lincolnton, N. C.

HARRY E. KRAMER
Whiteville, N. C.
Φ Α

W. LEROY KISER
Bessemer City,
N. C.

W. H. KURALT
Springfield, Mass.
Taylor Society.

KATE P. KITCHEN
Scotland Neck,
N. C.
Χ Ω

HELEN F. LANCE
Timberlake, N. C.

[132]

B. B. Lane, Jr.
Chapel, Hill, N. C.
Θ X

E. Duvall Lennon
Lumberton, N. C.
Yackety Yack Staff;
Buccaneer Staff.

X Φ

William H. Lane
Stantonsburg, N. C.
Θ Φ

W. S. Lindsay
Camden, S. C.
K A

Mebane T. Lea
Wilson, N. C.
Σ Z

Julius D. Linker
Salisbury, N. C.
Di Senate; Glee Club;
Boxing Squad.

Ludie Carrie Lee
Benson, N. C.

E. R. Lipscomb
Greensboro, N. C.

Vice-President Freshman
Class; Assistant Leade:
Sophomore Hop; Mino-
taurs; Football; Mono-
gram Club.

Σ X

Percy O. Leggett
Scotland Neck,
N. C.

Howard Q. Little
Conover, N. C.

JAMES M. LITTLE
Winston-Salem,
N. C.

EDITH H. MANGUM
Lexington, N. C.
Π B Φ

JOHN H. LONDON
Pittsboro, N. C.
Cabin.
Σ A E

A. S. MANN, JR.
Elizabeth City,
N. C.
Φ Σ K

L. F. LONDON
Pittsboro, N. C.
Cabin.
Σ A E

I. H. MANNING, JR.
Chapel Hill, N. C.

Y. M. C. A. Cabinet;
Varsity Track Squad;
Varsity Cross Country
Squad; Grail; German
Club; Commencement
Marshal; Business Staff
Buccaneer.

Φ K Σ

C. J. MADRY
Scotland Neck,
N. C.

ARTHUR R. MARPET
Yonkers, N. Y.

Freshman Basketball;
Freshman Baseball; Vice-
President Junior Class;
Monogram Club; Varsity
Basketball.

T E Φ

W. O. MANBECK
Cleveland Heights,
Ohio

Vice-President Taylor
Society.

Δ T Δ

A. A. MARSHALL
Wilmington, N. C.
Glee Club; Buccaneer.
Δ Σ Φ

A. Hugh Martin
Fairmont, W. Va.
Π K Φ

H. S. Merrell
Fairview, N. C.
Σ Φ E

C. O. Matthews
Kernersville, N. C.
Φ K Δ

Paul M. Michael
Kernersville, N. C.

Kay Kyser's Orchestra;
Band; Symphony Or-
chestra; Glee Club; Caro-
lina Tar Heels; Paul
Michael and His Or
chestra; Assistant Editor
Alumni Review.

P. W. Mattocks
Gillett, N. C.

Bonner S. Mills
Greenville, S. C.

Palmetto Club.

Σ X, A K Ψ

Clyde D. Mauney
Cherryville, N. C.

W. R. Mills, Jr.
Louisburg, N. C.
Φ Δ Θ

Carl W. Meares
Fair Bluff, N. C.

Debating Squad.

James R. Mohorn
Littleton, N. C.

[135]

ALBERT R. MONROE
Salisbury, N. C.

REEME MOORE
Dallas, Tex.

Δ Δ Δ

C. STOWE MOODY
Charlotte, N. C.

Tar Heel Staff; Inter-
fraternity Council; Ger-
man Club.

Π K A

RICHARD H. MOORE
Battleboro, N. C.

William Cain Society of
Civil Engineers; Wres-
tling; Monogram Club.

GEORGE D. MOODY
Charlotte, N. C.

B Θ Π

W. B. MOORE
Reidsville, N. C.

BEVERLY C. MOORE
Greensboro, N. C.

Secretary Sophomore
Class; Di Senate; Ger-
man Club; Mary D.
Wright Debate Medal;
Y. M. C. A. Cabinet;
Assistant Editor Tar
Heel.

Π K Φ, E Φ Δ

W. W. MOORE
Rocky Mount,
N. C.

Γ. H. J. MOORE
Stantonsburg, N. C.

Θ Φ

ROSCOE H. MORGAN
Marshville, N. C.

Holt Scholarship; Di
Senate.

EDNA MORRISETTE
Elizabeth City,
N. C.

X Ω

ROY McGINNIS
Gastonia, N. C.

Δ Θ Φ

ALFRED A. MOUNT
College Point, N.Y.
Rifle Club.

Σ Φ Σ, Δ Σ Π

W. H. McGLAMERY
Greensboro, N. C.

Φ Σ K

RALPH H. MUNCH
Chapel Hill, N. C.

A X Σ

C. B. MacKETHAN
Fayetteville, N. C.

Davidson College; Sports
Editor Tar Heel; Buc-
caneer; Phi Assembly;
Debating Society.

X Φ, A K Ψ

ADELAIDE McANALLY
High Point, N. C.

Π B Φ

OLLEN D. McLEOD
Raleigh, N. C.

Π K Φ

S. McCONNELL, JR.
Waterhouse, N. Y.

Assistant Leader Junior
Prom; Sheiks; Football
Squad; German Club.

Z Ψ

W. P. McPHERSON
Raleigh, N. C.

Z Ψ

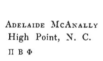
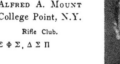

C. F. McRae
Chapel Hill, N. C.

G. F. Newman, Jr.
Greensboro, N. C.

Buccaneer Business Staff;
Assistant Manager Track;
German Club.

Π Κ Φ, Α Κ Ψ

S. L. Nathan
Mt. Vernon, N. Y.

T E Φ

Jesse S. Newsom
Sandersville, Ga.

Mechanical Engineers So-
ciety; Boxing Squad.

Θ Φ

Alferdo Nazareno
Philippines

Ε Φ Δ

Mary C. Norcross
Smithfield, N. C.

Χ Ω

David Neiman
Charlotte, N. C.

Varsity Basketball; Var-
sity Track.

T E Φ

W. H. Norman
Raleigh, N. C.

Χ Ψ

H. A. Nelson
Oak Park, Ill.

A. S. C. E.; Freshman
Football; Varsity Foot-
ball.

Α Τ Ω

Elton S. Oakes
Chapel Hill, N. C.

Dialectic Senate;
A. I. E. E.

GEORGE M. OLIVER
Yanceyville, N. C.
Freshman Football; Var-
sity Football.

P. G. PADGETT
Forest City, N. C.
Λ Χ Α

WILLIAM B. OLIVER
Pine Level, N. C.
Κ Α

RUFUS S. PARET
New York, N. Y.

C. B. OVERMAN
Washington, D. C.
Θ Φ

MILTON P. PARK
Greensboro, N. C.
Σ Ζ

R. S. OVERMAN
High Point, N. C.
Κ Σ

R. A. PARSLEY, JR.
Wilmington, N. C.
Dialectic Senate; Fresh-
man Football; Varsity
Football; Coop; German
Club; Grail; Gimghoul.
Σ Α Ε

D. J. PACHMAN
Brooklyn, N. Y.
Ζ Β Τ

E. L. PATTERSON
Statesville, N. C.
Cabin; German Club.
Π Κ Α

W. B. PATTERSON
Rochester, N. Y.

German Club.

E. C. PERSON, JR.
Pikeville, N. C.

Cabin; Minotaurs;
Gorgon's Head.

Σ N

H. N. PATTERSON
High Point, N. C.

Student Council, (2);
Business Manager Buc-
caneer, (3); Tar Heel
Business Staff, (1,
2); Y. M. C. A. Cab-
inet; Treasurer Dialectic
Senate, (3); Junior Class
Executive Committee;
Coop; Grail.

Φ Γ Δ, A K Ψ

Eugene E. Pfaff
Pfaffton, N. C.

B. E. PAXTON
Greenville, S. C.

Δ Ψ

Florence Phillips
Fredericksburg, Va.

A. G. PEELER, JR.
Salisbury, N. C.

X Φ

C. E. Pleasants
Winston-Salem,
N. C.

Π K Φ, A K Ψ

Alton W. Perry
Washington, N. C.

R. C. Plummer
Wilmington, N. C.

Θ Φ

R. H. PLUMMER
Brevard, N. C.

Π Κ Α

KERR C. RAMSAY
Salisbury, N. C.

Sub-Assistant Manager
Football; Sub-Assistant
Manager Track; Y. M.
C. A. Cabinet; Dialectic
Senate; City Editor Tar
Heel, (3); Elisha Mit-
chell Scientific Society;
German Club.

Σ Ν, Ε Φ Δ

R. L. POPLIN
Statesville, N. C.

Λ Χ Σ

MARSHALL D. RAND
Garner, N. C.

Freshman Baseball; Var-
sity Baseball; Monogram
Club.

Π Κ Φ

JOHN A. PREVOST
Waynesville, N. C.

Yackety Yack Business
Staff; German Club.

Λ Χ Α

ELIZABETH REED
Beaumont, Tex.

R. H. PROCTOR, JR.
Hollis, N. Y.

Φ Σ Κ

MARY A. REED
Beaumont, Tex.

Π Β Φ

GEORGE J. QUINN
East Orange, N. J.

Α Τ Ω

ROBERT REEVES
Cincinnati, Ohio

Χ Ψ

A. E. Reynolds, Jr.
Salisbury, N. C.
Φ Γ Δ

A. C. Robertson
Burlington, N. C.

Albert M. Rhett
Charleston, S. C.
Σ A E

G. P. Rosemond
Kinston, N. C.
K Σ

Paul H. Rhodes
Albemarle, N. C.

A. Rosenblatt
Brooklyn, N. Y.

T. M. Riddick
Gatesville, N. C.
Σ Ψ

Jamie H. Ross
Ayden, N. C.

George H. Roach
Greensboro, N. C.
Δ Σ Π

Ezra W. Rowe
Leakville, N. C.

[142]

C. L. ROYSTER
Chapel Hill, N. C.

Assistant Manager Bas-
ketball; Commencement
Marshal; "13" Club;
Gorgon's Head.

Σ Χ

SIDNEY W. SAYRE
Tryon, N. C.

RAYMOND J. RUBLE
Chapel Hill, N. C.

W. B. SCALES
Salisbury, N. C.

Δ Τ Δ

PETER B. RUFFIN
Wilmington, N. C.

Assistant Manager Foot-
ball; Coop; German
Club; Sheiks; Gimghoul.

Σ A E

JACK B. SCHNEIDER
Brooklyn, N. Y.

FLETCHER D. SAIN
Lawndale, N. C.

ERWIN R. SCOTT
Cummington, Mass.

Elisha Mitchell Scientific
Society.

ANDREW T. SAWYER
Elizabeth City,
N. C.

Π Κ A

EMIL N. SHAFFNER
Winston-Salem,
N. C.

Δ Τ Δ

[143]

H. L. Shaner, Jr.
Winston-Salem
N. C.

Π Κ Α

W. A. Sherrill
Granite Falls, N.C.

William G. Sheets
Winston-Salem,
N. C.

James R. Shirley
Swannanoa, N. C.

J. H. Sheffield
Canton, N. C.

Freshman Boxing; Varsity Boxing; Monogram Club.

Σ Z

A. deL. Sickles
Rochester, N. Y.

Assistant Manager Baseball; Freshman Basketball; Freshman Y. M. C. A. Cabinet; Wigue and Masque; Playmakers; Blue Key; Assistant Leader Mid-Winter Dances, (3); German Club.

Σ Χ, Α Κ Ψ

W. A. Shelton
Mt. Airy, N. C.

Α Α Τ

Byron A. Sieder
South Orange, N.J.

Α Τ Ω

Philip Sher
Durham, N. C.

Freshman Football; Freshman Basketball; Freshman Baseball; Varsity Basketball; Varsity Baseball; Monogram Club.

Τ Ε Φ

Charles C. Sikes
Monroe, N. C.

Σ Ν

S. L. Silverstein
Rockingham, N. C.

Y. M. C. A. Cabinet;
Yackety Yack Business
Staff; Manager Fresh-
man Baseball, (3).

Φ A

Budd E. Smith
Benson, N. C.

Wilfred N. Sisk
Raleigh, N. C.

Phi Assembly; Glee
Club; Elisha Mitchell
Scientific Society.

Claude A. Smith
Asheboro, N. C.

Leo B. Skeen
Biscoe, N. C.

Σ Z

Jack W. Smith
Wilmington, N. C.

Σ E

C. C. Skinner
Greenville, N. C.

Freshman Track; Var-
sity Track; Coop; Mino-
taurs; Commencement
Marshal; German Club.

Σ N, A K Ψ

Mattie D. Snider
Robbinsville, N. C.

John G. Slater
New Bern, N. C.

Basketball; Grail.

Π K Φ

William B. Snow
Asheville, N. C.

Z Ψ

[145]

D. M. SNYDER
Hamlet, N. C.

F. P. SPRUILL, JR.
Rocky Mount, N.C.

Y. M. C. A. Cabinet;
Glee Club; Playmakers;
Cabin.

Φ Κ Σ

C. G. SOUTHARD
Stokesdale, N. C.

E. H. STALLINGS
Enfield, N. C.

PHILIP SOWERS
Salisbury, N. C.

Α Λ Τ

W. A. STARBUCK
Winston-Salem,
N. C.

Δ Σ Φ

PAUL R. SPARKS
Burlington, N. J.

Σ Ε

JOSEPH B. STEIN
Fayetteville, N. C.

W. F. SPRAGUE
Chicago, Ill.

S. B. STERNBERGER
Wilmington, N. C.

Z Β Τ

JOHN H. STEWART
Greensboro, N. C.
Glee Club.

EVERETTE L. SWAIN
Walkertown, N. Y.
Φ Κ Δ

RICHARD L. SUGG
Southern Pines,
N. C.

WILLIAM S. TABB
Wilmington, N. C.
Freshman Football; Varsity Football; Monogram Club.

GEORGE R. SULKIN
Mattapan, Mass.
Buccaneer Staff; Orchestra; Band; Transfer from R. I. State.
Τ Ε Φ

JOHN T. TALLEY
New Hill, N. C.

HARDY A. SULLIVAN
Winter Garden,
Fla.

HUBER T. TAYLOR
Como, N. C.
Y. M. C. A. Cabinet.

ALBERT E. SUSKIN
New Bern, N. C.

THOMAS J. TAYLOR
Enfield, N. C.

1931

EDWARD F. THOMAS
Bainbridge, Ga.
Θ Χ, Α Χ Σ

MARION B. THOMAS
Talladega, Ala.
Transfer Howard
College.
Σ Ν

FRED A. THOMAS
Ramseur, N. C.
Δ Σ Φ

G. D. THOMPSON
Goldsboro, N. C.
Varsity Wrestling:
Monogram Club; Com-
mencement Marshal;
German Club.
Ζ Ψ

FRED C. THOMAS
Siler City, N. C.
Φ Σ Κ

W. C. THOMPSON
Rosemary, N. C.
U. N. C. Band; Or-
chestra; Jack Wardlaw
and His Orchestra.
Δ Σ Π

HENRY C. THOMAS
Charleston, S. C.
Α Χ Σ

W. S. THOMSON
Atlanta, Ga.
Σ Α Ε

JOHN L. THOMAS
Reidsville, N. C.

J. R. TOMLINSON
North Wilkesboro,
N. C.

VIRGINIA TURNER
Weldon, N. C.
Π Β Φ

WILLIAM R. WALL
Tobaccoville, N. C.

JAMES W. VANN
Salemburg, N. C.

J. McC. WARREN
Washington, N. C.

Freshman Boxing; Varsity Boxing; Varsity Football; Monogram Club.

JOHN S. VAUGHAN
Woodland, N. C.
Θ Κ Ν

JOHN S. WEATHERS
Ocala, Fla.

J. G. WADSWORTH
Williamston, N. C.

A. S. C. E.; German Club.

Σ Ν

ROY B. WEBB
Stantonsburg, N. C.

ROGER I. WALL
Wendell, N. C.

C. J. WEEKS
Whitakers, N. C.

Assistant Manager Boxing; Secretary Junior Class; German Club.

KERMIT WHEARY
Crewe, Va.

Associate Editor Bucca-
neer; Cabin.

Δ T Δ

RANKIN J. WHITE
Chapel Hill, N. C.

Σ Z

RUTH E. WHEATON
Ogdensburg, N. Y.

Π Β Φ

B. U. WHITEHEAD
Woodville, N. C.

Z Ψ

H. P. WHISNANT
Belmont, N. C.

Dialectic Senate; Fresh-
man Football; Gaston
County Club.

Σ Z

ILEY C. WHITELEY
Morganton, N. C.

ROY G. WHITAKER
Chapel Hill, N. C.

R. V. WHITENER
High Point, N. C.

C. L. WHITE, JR.
Concord, N. C.

Yackety Yack Staff;
Cabin.

Φ Γ Δ

DOWD P. WHITLEY
Monroe, N. C.

Σ E

W. R. WHITTENTON
Benson, N. C.

P. C. WIMBISH
Greensboro, N. C.
Π K Φ

R. J. WILKERSON
Roxboro, N. C.

G. T. WINSTON
Chapel Hill, N. C.
Φ K Σ

RUTH E. WILLIAMS
Morven, N. C.

MARY L. WITHERS
Raleigh, N. C.
Π B Φ

MEADE WILLIS
Winston-Salem,
N. C.

Sub-Assistant Manager
Baseball; Golf Team;
Minotaurs.

Δ K E

MAURICE WOLFE
Brooklyn, N. Y.

Freshman Football;
Freshman Tennis; Ata
Romani Club.

H. B. WILSON
Lenoir, N. C.

Glee Club; U. N. C.
Band; Carolina Tar Heel
· Orchestra.

Θ K N

DONALD L. WOOD
Kinston, N. C.

Glee Club; Tar Heel
Staff; Yackety Yack
Staff; Phi Assembly;
Freshman Inter-collegiate
Debate; Inter-society De-
bating; Y. M. C. A.
Cabinet; Le Cercle
Francais; Black and
White Revue; Wigue
and Masque.

Φ Σ K

EDWARD J. WOOD
Wilmington, N. C.

Σ A E

C. L. WYRICK
Greensboro, N. C.

Freshman Football and
Baseball; Varsity Foot-
ball and Baseball; Mono-
gram Club; President
Sophomore Class, (2);
Executive Committee
Junior Class.

Θ K N

C. K. WOODWARD
Greenville, N. C.

A T Ω

W. H. YARBOROUGH
Louisburg, N. C.

Sports Editor Tar Heel,
(1); Assistant Editor
Tar Heel, (2); Manag-
ing Editor Tar Heel,
(3); Sports Editor Yack-
ety Yack, (2); President
Publications Union
Board, (2); Dialectic
Senate; Junior Class Ex-
ecutive Committee; Sec-
retary and Treasurer
German Club, (3); Ger-
man Club: Coop: Sheiks;
German Club Executive
Committee.

Σ A E

H. V. WORTH, JR.
Raleigh, N. C.

Freshman Friendship
Council; Phi Assembly;
Circulation Manager Tar
Heel; Circulation Man-
ager Buccaneer; Yackety
Yack Staff, (2).

Σ A E

E. D. YEOMANS
Washington, D. C.

ERNEST H. WYCHE
Greensboro, N. C.

A X Σ

WILEY R. YOUNG
Angier, N. C.

The Little Emperor

SOPHOMORES

AYCOCK

SLUSSER

MILLER

BROWN

WALL

Officers of the Sophomore Class

BENJAMIN T. AYCOCK..President

FRANK W. SLUSSER..Vice-President

JOHN E. MILLER..Secretary

ROYAL R. BROWN..Treasurer

CRAIG WALL ....Student Councilman

Abelson, S. B.	Austin, C. M.	Bell, K. A.
Abernathy, J. M.	Austin, S. H.	Bell, W. M.
Adams, S.	Avery, R. H.	Belton, E. C.
Aderholdt, J. C.	Aycock, B. T.	Benoit, H. B.
Alexander, T. W.	Badger, T.	Best, G. E.
Alford, G. H.	Baldwin, B. T.	Bevacqua, A. E.
Allen, A. N.	Barber, B. G.	Bissell, W. N.
Allen, L. M.	Barfield, W. C.	Blake, R. B.
Allison, H. C.	Barham, S. A.	Bliss, W. M.
Alphin, R. L.	Barkley, C. V.	Blythe, C. E.
Alston, P. K.	Barnes, H. M.	Boatwright, S. M.
Anderson, H. L.	Barnes, J. D.	Boger, W. G.
Andrews, C. M.	Baroody, T. A.	Booth, J. W.
Andrews, J.	Barrett, J. F.	Boren, A. C.
Angotti, S. A.	Bartlett, G. L.	Boring, H. W.
Armfield, J. W.	Bass, J. L.	Bowman, H. G.
Armfield, R. B.	Bateman, S. J.	Bowman, N. O.
Askew, D. E.	Battley, W. R.	Boyd, C. H.
Atkinson, W. M.	Beacham, G. A.	Boynton, W. L.
Atiyeh, F. E.	Beam, B. F.	Branch, J. D.
Auman, H. F.	Beaman, J. W.	Brawley, R. M.

Breen, S. J.
Breene, J. G.
Bremer, T. W.
Brewer, E. F.
Bridgers, W. A.
Briggs, V. L.
Brooker, L. P.
Brooks, T. H.
Brown, A. C., Jr.
Brown, A. C.
Brown, R. R.
Brown, T. R.
Brown, W. G.
Bryan, N. E.
Bryan, W. D.
Bryant, E. O.
Buie, J. M.
Bunn, J. P.
Burch, L. D.
Burnett, R. T.
Burwell, R. G.
Campbell, R. H.
Campbell, T. J.
Cannon, R. L.
Carmichael, D. M.
Carpenter, J. H.
Carr, A. B.
Carter, P. S.
Carter, S. R.
Carver, F. O.
Case, W. T.
Chace, R. A.
Chamberlain, F. H., Jr.
Chamberlain, R. M.
Chaoush, E.
Cheek, C. C.
Clark, S. L.
Clary, M. S.
Clifton, D. H.
Clinard, J. W.
Coats, G. H.
Coburn, R. T.
Cochrane, G. C.
Cohen, R.
Cohen, S. P.
Coker, R. E.
Cole, F. A., Jr.
Connally, J. C.
Connally, W. E.

Conrad, E. V.
Cooke, D. P.
Cook, J. L.
Cooper, J. P.
Cooper, P. S.
Cornwall, C. C.
Cowper, A. W.
Cozart, S. M.
Craig, J. C.
Crawford, W. S.
Crawford, W. C.
Crook, C. V.
Crouch, W. M.
Crutchfield, W. T.
Culbreth, W. H.
Currie, J. A.
Dalton, L. A.
Daniel, A. N.
Daniel, J. W.
Dannenbaum, G.
Dannenbaum, R.
Davis, B. W.
Davis, J. E.
Davis, J. H.
Davis, T. P.
Dawson, J. B.
Deaton, R. L.
Denning, J. R.
Devereaux, J. I.
Dewar, N. T.
Dickinson, J. L.
Dillehay, H. J.
Doster, L. C.
Daughton, J. E.
Douglas, A. E.
Downing, C. D.
Draper, W. F.
Dratler, J. J.
Dresslar, O. W.
Duls, J. M.
Dunbar, A. W.
Duncan, O. E.
Dunevant, S. J.
Dungan, J. E.
Dunlap, F. B.
Dunn, F. H.
Dunning, W. L.
Eagles, R. L.
Edwards, D. C.

Edwards, J. P.
Edwards, W. W.
Efird, J. E.
Egan, E. G.
Eighme, M. E.
Eisenburg, E. E.
Eliason, A. H.
Elkins, C. H.
Ellege, C. C.
Elliot, R. W.
Ellison, J. B.
Elson, J. R.
Everett, W. A.
Farmer, C. M.
Farrell, F. W.
Farris, J. B.
Felton, L. J.
Fender, R.
Fillman, J. B.
Finch, H. C.
Fitch, M. M.
Fleming, A. H., Jr.
Fleming, S. W.
Fleming-Jones, J. M.
Flinn, L.
Flowers, W. A.
Folger, B. F.
Follin, T. B.
Fonvielle, E. M.
Forney, T. J.
Foster, D. R.
Fowler, E. M.
French, G. E.
French, G. E., Jr.
Frisby, E. F.
Furr, E. M.
Garner, F. M.
Gatling, J. M.
Geitner, R. W.
Gentry, B. G.
Gibbons, H. E.
Gilbreath, J. U.
Gilchrist, P. S.
Gill, E. D.
Gillespie, J. M.
Ginn, J. T.
Glenn, E. T.
Glenn, M. S.
Glover, F. M.

Goebel, R. W.	Guthrie, C. H.	Houston, G. P.
Godwin, R. C.	Guthrie, P. H.	Howe, C. K.
Goode, J. F.	Hall, W. K.	Hudson, J. A.
Goodes, B. L.	Hamilton, J. deR.	Huff, H. J.
Goodman, J. V.	Hampton, K. D.	Huffman, J. E.
Gordon, J. W.	Hancock, C. C.	Hughes, D. G.
Graham, E. K.	Hanna, R. E.	Humphries, W. F.
Gray, F.	Hanscome, C. R.	Hunt, O. S.
Gray, M.	Harper, J. P.	Hunter, J. L.
Greer, F. B.	Harris, J. L.	Hutchison, J. J.
Gregory, H. T.	Harris, L. R.	Isenhour, J. H.
Gregory, J. F.	Heffelfinger, W. W.	Jackson, L. F.
Grier, B. K.	Heffner, B. L.	Jackson, M. W.
Griffin, A. T.	Henderson, R.	James, F. M.
Griffin, I. C., Jr.	Henlin, H. H.	Jameson, H.
Griggs, C. F.	Hines, H.	Jarman, W. H.
Groome, I. A.	Hirsh, S. L.	Jenkins, R. T.
Gross, E. T.	Hobgood, H. H.	Jernigan, L. B.
Grover, E. M.	Hodges, R. M.	Jenrette, T. S.
Gump, H.	Hooks, L. D.	Johnson, C. B.
Gupton, L. O.	Horney, G. F.	Johnson, D. C.

Johnson, F. K.
Johnson, L. B.
Johnson, P. H.
Johnson, R. G.
Johnson, T. L., Jr.
Johnson, W. B.
Johnson, W. W.
Jones, G. L.
Jones, H. F., Jr.
Kapp, C. H.
Kaufman, A. W.
Keim, G. C.
Keller, W. L.
Kendrick, E. L.
Kennedy, J. H., Jr.
Kenyon, V. L.
Kerr, J. W.
Kersey, W. R.
Ketchie, H. D.
Kidd, E. B., Jr.
Kindel, W. A.
King, E. W.
King, F. L., Jr.
Kiser, A. G.
Kjellesvig, K. L.
Kleemeier, J. A., Jr.
Klein, M. B.
Knoop, F., Jr.
Kochtitzky, O. W., Jr.
Koonce, C. H.
Kresky, M.
Krauss, F. C.
Krider, J. H.
Kushner, R. L.
Kyles, P.
Lancaster, W. L.
Latta, H. C., Jr.
Lawson, C. F.
Layton, J. S.
Lea, S. L. W.
Lee, P. G.
Lefler, A. L.
Leibowitz, A.
Lentz, P. J.
Levitt, R. O.
Lewis, F. G.
Liberstein, W.
Liles, G. A.
Lilly, H. M.

Little, A. D.
London, H. M.
Long, J. W.
Longest, E. C.
Love, M. S.
Loveland, L. J.
Loven, A. W.
Lowrance, L. H.
Lynch, S. A., Jr.
McAlister, J. W.
McLure, D. C.
McDaniel, M. T.
McGraw, F. G.
McIver, H. S.
McKinnon, E. H.
McLaughlin, T. L.
McLean, E. P.
McLeod, M. M.
McMichael, J.
McMinis, W. C.
McNairy, J. D.
McRae, C. F.
Madry, J. D.
Mann, E. S.
Manning, E. H.
Manning, H. S.
Marland, K. M.
Marley, W. M.
Marreale, L.
Marsh, S. P.
Marshall, R. W.
Marshall, T. E., Jr.
Martin, A. H.
Mason, W. L.
Mathews, M. M.
Mattocks, P. W.
Meares, L. A.
MeHaffey, J. P.
Mewborne, J. F.
Meyers, H.
Midgett, E. L.
Midgett, L. W.
Miller, H. R.
Miller, J. E.
Miller, J. H.
Miller, J. M.
Miller, L. L.
Millikan, T. W.
Mitchell, A. J.

Mock, C. G.
Moore, A. L.
Moore, J. O.
Moore, J. O.
Moore, L. W.
Mooring, H. B.
Morris, J. F.
Morrison, J. S.
Moseley, H. E.
Moser, R. L.
Muse, C. M.
Myers, W. T.
Neville, B. H.
Norman, J. H., III
O'Donnell, H. H.
Olmstead, W. F.
Overby, D. R.
Owens, F. N.
Paddison, A. H.
Park, J. A., Jr.
Parrish, R. B.
Parrish, W. L.
Parsons, T. L.
Peace, S. T.
Pearlstine, F. J.
Pearson, T. G., Jr.
Peele, J. C.
Perkins, A. R., Jr.
Perlmutter, J.
Peschau, J., Jr.
Petty, W. C.
Phillips, A. A.
Phoenix, C. B.
Pierce, G. N.
Pittman, F. W.
Pond, R. C.
Poplin, R. W.
Powell, E. C.
Preston, J. A.
Pretlow, J. C., Jr.
Prouty, F. M.
Purser, J. C.
Quinn, R. C.
Rader, C. M., Jr.
Rawles, T. C.
Raymer, D.
Reavis, C. W.
Redding, R. L.
Redding, T. H.

[1 5 8]

Reid, W. G.	Sale, L. W.	Shields, J. D.
Remsen, O. C.	Sample, F. L.	Shore, J. S.
Rhyne, A. L.	Sams, R. L.	Shreve, C. A.
Ritchie, B. L.	Sanders, G. C., Jr.	Silver, O. K.
Roberts, D. B.	Sartwell, R. T.	Sitterson, J. C.
Roberts, R. H.	Satterfield, W. R.	Skinner, J. G.
Roberts, R. J.	Schnell, R. H.	Skinner, W. I.
Robertson, A. C.	Schultz, G. L.	Slaughter, J. W.
Robinson, W. D.	Schwitz, P. R.	Slusser, F. W.
Rodwell, W. P.	Scoggin, L. E.	Smathers, F.
Rogen, T. C., Jr.	Sechler, N. A.	Smith, H. E.
Rollins, C. D.	Shachtman, J. M.	Smith, J. G.
Rose, W. T.	Shapiro, S. I.	Smith, J. W.
Rosenfield, M. A.	Sharpe, P. L.	Smith, P. H.
Ross, J. D.	Shedd, W. B.	Sosnick, N. Y.
Ross, M. L.	Shelton, T. M., Jr.	Southard, H. J.
Rosser, T. R.	Shepard, F. A.	Southerland, F., Jr.
Ruehl, V. E.	Sherfesee, L., Jr.	Southerland, W. O.
Ruffin, T.	Sherrill, J. L.	Spell, J. B.
Rulfs, D. J.	Sherrill, J. P.	Spitzer, L. L.
Sachs, I. W.	Shevick, B. B.	Stahr, A. L.

Stallings, G. M.
Stallings, J. W.
Starnes, H. W.
Stoute, R. D.
Stovall, R. G.
Strawn, J. B.
Strickland, B. E.
Strickland, W. L.
Strusinski, J. R.
Stuart, C. K.
Stubbs, C. A.
Stultz, H. J.
Sturm, G. H.
Sungaard, A.
Suther, J. A.
Tatum, C. C.
Taylor, A. H.
Taylor, C. E.
Taylor, C. W.
Taylor, G. S.
Taylor, H. H., Jr.
Taylor, J. Y.
Taylor, W. R., Jr.
Taylor, W. W.
Teachey, J. C., Jr.
Teer, T. W.
Temple, R. H.
Thomas, A. J.
Thomas, G. W., Jr.
Thomas, J. L.
Thomas, J. L., Jr.
Thompson, G. W.
Thompson, N. A.
Thurston, D. J., Jr.
Tillery, P. A.
Timberlake, S. D.
Tinkham, M. F.

Todd, C. L.
Tomlinson, W. S.
Toole, A. F.
Torbert, J. F.
Triplett, H. C.
Triplett, K. D.
Trott, G. F.
Trull, G. I.
Tsumas, H. P.
Tucker, C. M., Jr.
Tunstan, K. R.
Turchiarelli, S. V.
Turner, H. F.
Tyson, J. P.
Umstead, E. V.
Underwood, N. A.
Upshaw, S. H.
Usher, P. C.
Uzzell, W. E.
Van Echop, G. L.
Vinson, H.
Voss, J.
Walker, A. S.
Walker, E. N.
Wall, C. E.
Wall, J. E., Jr.
Wall, J. G.
Wall, J. S.
Walters, J. D.
Ward, H. G.
Wardlaw, C. D. Jr.
Wardlaw, F. C.
Ware, G. H.
Warlick, G. L.
Waterhouse, G.
Waugh, D. B.
Weaver, I. V.

Weaver, J. R.
Webb, M. A.
Webb, T. N.
Weeks, G. L.
Weeks, O. H.
Weeks, T. W.
Weil, L. S.
Weinstein, R. L.
Wells, L. T.
West, C. R.
West, G. E.
Wheatley, J. R.
Whedbee, C. H.
Whisnant, W. D.
White, J. S., Jr.
Whitsett, W. T., Jr.
Whittington, E. M., Jr.
Whittington, R. J., Jr.
Whitton, B.
Wiggins, N. E.
Wilburn, G.
Wilder, L.
Wilkinson, J. A.
Williams, J. S.
Wilson, K. C.
Wilson, M. A.
Wilson, M. B.
Wilson, W. T.
Winstead, S. B.
Withers, W. A.
Woodard, N. B.
Woodley, B. W.
Yancey, S. M.
Yarborough, E. F.
Young, O. J.
Zachary, C. R.
Zagora, E. J.

The Invasion

FRESHMEN

YACKETY YACK

HUBBARD

JENSEN

LONDON

PEACOCK

Officers of the Freshman Class

JAMES R. HUBBARD..President

GEORGE E. LONDON..................................Vice-President

CLARENCE A. JENSEN................................Secretary

JOHN G. PEACOCK..Treasurer

Abels, L. C.	Atwood, R. C.	Beale, S. M.	Bonner, N. J.
Abernathy, R. O.	Auman, J. M.	Beale, W. E.	Bontamase, J.
Abernathy, W. E.	Auman, L. W.	Beam, D. P.	Boone, E. T.
Abrams, S. H.	Autry, B.	Beam, H. F.	Bost, A. J.
Adams, J. B.	Aycock, M. E.	Beckham, T. T.	Boyd, H. A.
Adams, J. S.	Bacot, W. W.	Bender, F. T.	Bradley, C. L.
Adams, S. L., Jr.	Bailey, B. R.	Benjamin, A.	Braddy, H. C.
Adams, V. H.	Baird, J. L.	Bennett, F., Jr.	Brannon, C. B.
Adams, T. E.	Baker, A. L.	Bennett, G. F.	Brawley, C. H.
Adkins, T. F.	Baker, J. T.	Bessen, J.	Bray, B. B.
Aiken, C. H.	Ballenger, E. G.	Biggers, J. A.	Brenner, E.
Allen, B. H.	Barber, M. A.	Biggers, R. L.	Brett, H. F.
Allen, G. L.	Barham, D.	Biggs, A. G.	Bridger, H. C.
Allen, H. M.	Barnes, H.	Biggs, G. H.	Bridgers, J. K.
Allison, C. W.	Barnes, W. E.	Bisaner, E. A.	Brock, R. B.
Allsbrook, W. R.	Barnes, W. E.	Black, F. S.	Brooks, A. L., Jr.
Ames, N.	Barns, N. D.	Blackman, W. W.	Brooks, L. B.
Anderson, F. I.	Barnett, R. W.	Blackwood, I. S.	Brooks, R. E.
Angel, B. A.	Barnwell, G. G.	Blauman, G.	Brown, C. H., Jr.
Armstrong, W. E.	Barry, H. N.	Bloom, A.	Brown, G.
Arthur, B.	Beady, H. C.	Blue, J. A.	Brown, M. S.

Brown, M. Z.
Brown, V. L.
Bryson, H.
Buchanan, E. W.
Buchanan, R. A.
Buchanan, W. C.
Bunn, J. H.
Bunn, T. B.
Burdett, K. M.
Burnett, J. T.
Burrus, H. D.
Bynum, S.
Cain, F. C.
Caldwell, A. F.
Caldwell, R. S.
Cameron, M. T.
Cameron, N. C.
Campbell, C. L.
Campbell, P.
Campen, T. B.
Cantrell, C. H.
Carlton, C. W.
Carmichael, R. H.
Carpenter, S. W.
Carr, B.
Carr, C. S.
Cassada, H. H.
Cate, A. S.
Caveny, C. R.
Chandler, S. M.
Chatham, R. H.
Chears, V. T.
Civils, H. F.
Clapp, E. B.
Clark, J. A.
Clawson, F. D.
Click, H. F.
Coates, H. N.
Cockerham, V. Z.
Cole, A. V.
Collier, W. E.
Collins, J. W.
Colyer, J. F.
Cone, H. S.
Conklin, D. R.
Connor, H. G.
Cooper, F. B.
Cordle, T. L.
Couch, J. H.

Covington, R. L.
Covington, W. V.
Cowhig, R. K.
Cox, J. C.
Crane, T. P.
Crews, C. F.
Crews, J. W.
Croom, J. D.
Croom, W. D., Jr.
Crow, H. D.
Crowell, A. W.
Crowson, C. A.
Crum, C. F.
Crumpler, S. H.
Culpepper, E. M.
Curl, A. O., Jr.
Cuthrell, J. E.
Daley, C. C., Jr.
Daniel, C. G.
Daniel, E. A.
Daniel, E. C.
Daniel, J. W.
Daniels, O. C.
Daughtridge, U.
Dauthit, J. V.
Davidson, T. A.
Davis, A. B.
Davis, A. K.
Davis, C. W.
Davis, E. B.
Davis, F. P.
Davis, J. O.
Davis, M. F.
Davis, R. D.
Davis, W. T.
DeHart, C. R.
Deans, E. V.
Deans, J. L.
Deitz, C. J.
Dellinger, F. G.
Denton, T. E.
Dilda, S. L.
Dillard, J. E.
Dintsman, J.
Dixon, J. G.
Dixon, W. N.
Dodson, W. I.
Donnell, G. S.
Dozier, J. S.

Drane, R. W., Jr.
Drasner, J.
Dudley, E.
Dudley, G. A.
Dudley, J. W.
Dunn, J. E.
Dunn, R. W.
Dupree, F. T., Jr.
Durham, A. V.
Durham, L. W.
Edwards, K. F.
Edwards, T. R.
Edwards, W. E.
Eisner, J.
Errico, F. J.
Etheridge, V. B.
Evans, T. C.
Farmer, B. D.
Farrell, M. C.
Ferebee, E. C.
Ferguson, E. B.
Ferguson, R. S.
Ferell, J. F.
Fischer, J. L.
Fitzgerald, W. B.
Fitzgerald, W. C.
Fleming, R. G.
Fleishman, M.
Flusser, B. A.
Flynt, R. H.
Forbes, C. S.
Fountain, J. E.
Fowler, C. W.
Fox, C. D.
Fox, P. R.
Fraley, F. F.
Frasier, H. B.
Frazer, B. B.
Freeman, R. B.
Froneberger, R. E.
Fulcher, H. S.
Furchgott, A. C.
Gaither, M. Z.
Galloway, J. K.
Gant, J. E.
Garland, P. W.
Garren, N. M.
Gault, C. B.
Gaylord, A. L.

Geiger, J. F.
Gidney, R. S.
Gillies, R. M.
Glaberson, S. J.
Glascock, T. A., Jr.
Glenn, J. P.
Gobble, B. J.
Goodson, J. M.
Gorham, G. W.
Gorrell, J. S.
Grant, B.
Grantham, N. B.
Gray, D. E., Jr.
Gray, J. P.
Gray, W. L.
Greer, L. G.
Griffin, D. M.
Griffin, J. F.
Griffin, J. S.
Griffin, W. H.
Griffith, J. T.
Grotzman, H.
Haines, H. A., Jr.
Haislip, O. L.
Hamer, J. B.
Hamilton, A. T.
Hamilton, R. V.
Hamlet, C. C.
Hammond, W. L.
Hardy, R. T.
Hargreave, A. G.
Harper, W. B.
Harrell, D. A.
Harrell, R. H. S.
Harris, C. N.
Harris, W. E.
Hassell, T. C.
Hawkins, J. S.
Hawley, F. M.
Hayes, J. S.
Hayes, W. M.
Heafner, B. F.
Hedrick, P.
Helms, J. R.
Henry, C. C.
Henry, D. P.
Herkimer, B.
Hewitt, M. H.
Hewitt, W. W.

Hicks, A. M.	Holshouser, C. S.	Isbell, T. P.	Jones, W. E.
Higdon, E. D.	Holt, W. K.	Isley, J. M.	Jones, W. O.
Hill, J. P.	Hoover, W. L.	Jackson, C. C.	Justus, F. H.
Hiller, R. L.	Hornaday, F. D.	Jackson, J. W.	Karle, W. H.
Hinds, J. J.	Horne, J. R.	Jackson, C.	Kaufman, A.
Hine, G. H.	Houser, J. P.	Jackson, P. R.	Kaufman, P. K.
Hines, W. M.	Houser, W. H.	Jackson, S. D.	Keefe, J. E.
Hinkle, D. R.	Howard, W. A.	Jarratt, J. B.	Kelly, D. M.
Hinkle, W. L.	Howe, H. R.	Jeffreys, J. F.	Kenan, J. G.
Hinson, S. W.	Hubbard, J. R.	Jensen, C. A.	Kincaid, T. R.
Hocutt, H. Q.	Hubbard, R. B.	Johnson, C. E.	King, R. B.
Hodges, B. H.	Huff, R. D.	Johnson, L. L.	Kluttz, C. H.
Hodges, H. B.	Hughes, I. W.	Johnson, R. W.	Knowles, R.
Hodges, H. M.	Hughes, R. E.	Johnson, T. B.	Koch, F. H.
Hodges, R. T.	Hunter, C. E.	Johnson, W. W.	Kornegay, A. D.
Hoffman, W. R.	Hutchinson, J. C.	Johnston, A. H.	Kurfees, J. G.
Hogan, N. T.	Hyman, A.	Johnston, J. R.	Kyle, H. H.
Holcomb, C. E.	Idol, P. C.	Jones, C. C.	Landis, P. W.
Holland, J. S.	Ingold, G. F.	Jones, G. A.	Lane, W. A.
Holland, M. W.	Irvin, E. J.	Jones, M. M.	Lansford, A. M.
Holland, Y. L.	Irving, F. R.		Lassiter, J. H.

Lathan, B. W.
Latham, J. D.
Lawson, J. P.
Laxton, F. M.
Leary, H. A.
Lee, E. L., Jr.
Lee, H. M.
Leonard, C. W.
Leonard, F. A.
Lester, J. W.
Levinson, M.
Levy, T. D.
Lewis, J. C.
Lewis, W. E.
Lindy, A.
Lineberger, J. W.
Lingerfeldt, T. H.
Lloyd, W. L.
Loftin, C. I.
London, G. E.
Long, J. J.
Long, J. P.
Long, R. V.
Long, W. I.
Lubetkin, H. L.
Lucas, W. W.
Ludenan, R. D.
Lumpkin, N. W.
Lynch, J. M.
Lyon, W. H.
McAllister, H. C.
McArthur, W. S.
McCampbell, J. C.
McCaskill, J. H.
McCorkle, W. C.
McCoy, C. L.
McDade, R. A.
McDiarmid, D. A.
McDonald, H. J.
McDuffie, D. C.
McDuffie, W. C.
McGauley, J. J.
McGill, S. F.
McIllwaine, R. E.
McKee, W. W.
McLean, J. A.
McLean, M. A.
McLean, W. B.
McLellan, L. R.

McLeod, A. H.
McLeod, F. A.
McNeill, L. J.
Macon, W. C.
Madison, F. B.
Madison, R.
Manheim, F. J.
Mann, E. B.
Mann, C. S.
Manning, J. T.
Margolis, J. H.
Marguilies, I. M.
Markham, W. S.
Martin, R. T.
Martindale, H. S.
Marvel, E.
Marvin, J. R.
Mashburn, T. M.
Mason, R. H.
Massengill, W. W.
Mattocks, T. C.
Maybank, T.
Meacham, H. L.
Mebane, R. J.
Merritt, J. F.
Miller, W. A.
Miller, W. G.
Minsker, B. H.
Mintz, S.
Misenheimer, C. P.
Mitcham, W. C. Jr.
Mitchelle, W. E.
Mixson, S. J.
Mobley, C. W.
Moore, E. L.
Moore, M. B.
Moore, O. J.
Moore, W. H.
Moore, W. N.
Moorer, M. P.
Morgan, Z. V.
Morisey, J. C.
Morrison, M. S. Jr.
Moss, F. M.
Mowery, H. B.
Moye, J. M.
Murphy, G. S.
Nahakain, H. M.
Naylor, B.

Neal, W. A.
Newcombe, E. H.
Newland, H. T.
Newton, J. L. Jr.
Nichols, C. I.
Nichols, H. A.
O'Brien, W. J.
Oberfell, G. F.
Oden, W. A.
Olivirio, A. A.
Orbaugh, R. E.
Outlaw, M.
Overstreet, H.
Owen, O. C. Jr.
Palmer, A. T.
Parker, B. F.
Parker, J. E.
Parker, J. W.
Parker, W. M.
Parks, G. R.
Parrott, A.
Parsley, H. N.
Pate, W. M.
Patrick, B. F.
Patrick, C. L.
Patterson, C. J.
Patterson, F. G.
Patterson, W. B.
Pattisall, R. O.
Peacock, J. G.
Peacock, J. T.
Peacock, J. W.
Peacock, P. N.
Pearson, G. W.
Peeler, P. M.
Peetz, W. W.
Pelton, P. P., Jr.
Penn, C. A.
Peoples, C. C.
Peres, I. S.
Petree, W. S.
Petty, A. B.
Phillips, F. T.
Phillips, G. A.
Philpott, B. C.
Pickett, A. M.
Pickett, R. L.
Piland, N. E.
Poindexter, H. O.

Poole, R. W.
Porter, M. G.
Powell, A. V.
Powell, E. C.
Powell, W. C.
Powell, W. L.
Power, C. E.
Pratt, J. H.
Prince, B. C., Jr.
Prince, M.
Proctor, B. C.
Propst, W. G.
Rabinowitz, S.
Radford, G. E.
Ramsay, A. W.
Rankin, B. J.
Raper, J. R.
Ratcliffe, T. E.
Ray, F.
Rea, T. E.
Redding, T. S.
Redfern, B.
Redfern, R. A.
Reid, G.
Renegar, G. J.
Renn, C. A.
Reynolds, J. W. Jr.
Rice, I.
Richardson, L.
Riddle, R. B.
Ridenhour, W. B.
Riggs, L. D.
Riley, J. R.
Ritchie, H. R.
Rives, C. M.
Roberts, D. B.
Roberts, W. G.
Robey, W. M.
Robbins, J. C.
Robinson, C.
Robinson, E. T.
Robinson, W. A.
Rogers, C. P.
Rooch, R.
Rose, C. G.
Roseman, J. M. S.
Ross, L. W.
Roth, W. L.
Rouse, L. L.

Rowland, L. O.	Shemwell, E. B.	Smith, J. H.	Stinson, T. W.
Royster, T. S.	Shepherd, W. V.	Smith, J. H.	Stone, G. G.
Rubin, A.	Sherrill, J. A.	Smith, J. S.	Stone, M. F.
Sale, H. S.	Shlefstein, I. H.	Smith, W. L.	Stone, W. H.
Salley, M. C.	Shoemaker, J. R.	Snell, L. H.	Stowe, C. P.
Sandford, W. A.	Shuford, A. I.	Snider, A. H.	Strickland, J. F.
Sapp, R. E.	Shuford, J. A.	Spigel, J. N.	Strickland, W. S.
Savage, F. L.	Shuford, J. H.	Spradlin, W. H.	Studdert, R. S.
Sawyer, A.	Sickler, W. B.	Stafford, C. G.	Surprenant, L. C.
Sawyer, C. M.	Simmons, N. L.	Stallings, J. O.	Sutton, T. K.
Saylor, C.	Singletary, W. C.	Stallings, W. R.	Swann, T. F.
Scarboro, S. S.	Skinner, A. C.	Stanley, R. W.	Taylor, J. K.
Scarborough, V. H.	Skinner, L. C.	Stanley, W. H.	Taylor, S. N.
Schenck, S. C.	Slack, H. J.	Staples, E. W.	Taylor, T. R.
Seawell, D. R.	Slater, J. E.	Starnes, H. W.	Teachey, W.
Seglinson, E. N.	Sloop, J. D.	Staton, R. H.	Thomas, F. E.
Setser, A. L.	Small, H. R.	Steele, A. M.	Thomas, H. N.
Sewell, C. W.	Smith, A. P.	Steere, J. E.	Thomas, W. G.
Sewell, D. M.	Smith, D. H.	Stikeleather, J. G.	Thomasson, G. L.
Sharkey, J. P.	Smith, J. F.	Still, J. T.	Thompson, J.
Shelton, O. H.		Still, R. W.	

Thompson, J. B.
Thompson, K. L.
Thompson, P. M.
Tilford, P. P.
Toler, V. W.
Trimble, C. W.
Trotter, W. L.
Turner, L. C.
Urband, A.
Van Cleave, R. A.
Van Hoy, J. H.
Valk, A. deT.
Verburg, P. L.
Vick, G. R.
Vinson, A. S., Jr.
Volkman, N. H., Jr.
Walck, C. W.
Walker, E. G.
Walker, T. H.
Walker, W. W.
Wall, W. S.
Wanderman, I. L.
Ward, J. S.
Ward, S. A.

Ward, V. A.
Warnom, A. H.
Warren, R. T.
Warshaver, S. E.
Wasserman, J. L.
Watkins, T. H.
Watson, L. E.
Watson, T. S.
Weaver, G. B.
Webb, A.
Webb, G. L.
Weeks, C. S.
Weiland, H. J., Jr.
Weinberg, S. L.
Weinstein, M.
Weinstein, M. D.
Weis, G. O.
Wells, N. E.
Wescott, C. C.
West, J. L.
Westbrook, J. L.
White, K. T.
White, T. S.
White, W. F.

White, W. L.
Whitehart, G. L.
Whitehead, L. W.
Whitfield, R.
Widenhouse, J. W.
Wilder, J. F.
Wilkins, E. V.
Wilkinson, H. H.
Williams, B. B.
Williams, E. C.
Williams, J. R.
Williams, J. W.
Williams, S. W.
Williamson, O. G.
Williford, J. R.
Willis, E. C., Jr.
Wilson, G. W.
Wilson, H. M.
Wilson, W. H.
Winecoff, G. M.
Winig, B.
Winstead, C. C.
Winstead, J. D.
Withrow, E. J.

Witkins, B.
Wood, H., III
Wood, W. D.
Woodard, L. C.
Wornom, A. H.
Worrell, T. M.
Worseley, G. C.
Worth, T. C.
Wright, J. T.
Wright, K. O.
Wright, L. C.
Wright, T. H.
Yarborough, K. P.
Yarborough, R. F.
Yeomans, A. H.
Young, G. M.
Young, J. B.
Young, N. R.
Zaglin, J. G.
Zelley, H. N.
Zibelin, C. V.
Zovesus, A. J.

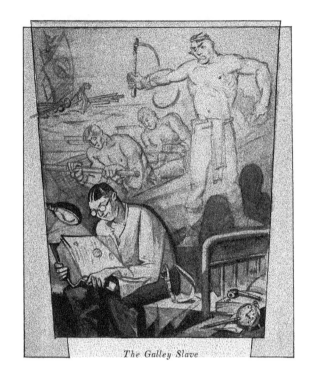

The Galley Slave

PROFESSIONAL

The Law School

The Law School

C. W. GHOLSON, JR...*President Law School Association*

Third Year Law Class

J. B. LEWIS...*President*

J. H. Anderson	A. B. Holmes	G. D. McDaniel	C. O. Sapp
E. O. Ayscue	W. Hoyle	J. B. McMullen	W. D. Sharpe, Jr.
H. Bane	W. S. Jenkins	G. C. Meads	A. K. Smith
A. M. Covington	J. B. Lewis	J. A. Mulligan	N. S. Sowers
A. T. Daniel	J. B. Linn	F. O. Parker	T. W. Sprinkle
B. Eaton, Jr.	B. T. Lord	F. A. Pollard	E. F. Taylor
J. F. Glenn	J. E. Magner	H. T. Powell	L. H. Wallace
A. W. Gholson	C. S. Mangum	H. Rockwell	M. P. Wilson

Second Year Law Class

J. H. CHADBOURN...*President*

P. B. Abbott	J. T. Edwards	W. S. Malone	G. A. Smith
K. Barwick	S. Felshin	R. McGinnis	T. C. Smith, Jr.
H. W. Blackstock	C. O'H. Grimes	H. B. Parker	Y. M. Smith
M. Bryson	J. E. Johnson	C. Price	K. W. Swartz
J. H. Chadbourn	M. Kellogg, Jr.	C. E. Reitzel, Jr.	T. A. Uzzell, Jr.
G. V. Cowper, Jr.	R. G. Key	H. Roane	A. T. Ward
E. L. Curlee	H. L. Lackey	E. L. Russell	J. A. Williams
R. Duffy	L. E. Lancaster	P. Roland	J. M. Wright
	G. E. Levings	E. Scheidt	

First Year Law Class

O. A. WARREN...*President*

J. G. Adams	D. J. Craig, Jr.	H. M. Kluttz	C. J. Shannon
M. R. Alexander	G. T. Davis	A. W. Langston	O. M. Smith
T. T. Brown	W. P. Fuller	H. L. Lobdell	P. J. Storey
M. S. Benton	T. J. Gold	G. A. Long	W. A. Stringfellow
G. P. Boucher	L. J. Giles, Jr.	W. L. Marshall, Jr.	A. J. Stubbs
J. D. Bulluck, Jr.	C. Graves, Jr.	S. G. Morse	D. E. Thomas
H. B. Campbell	R. M. Gray, Jr.	B. M. Parker	M. L. Thompson
C. C. Cates	F. D. Hamrick	T. B. Rector	H. N. Woodson
W. T. Covington, Jr.	E. A. Humphrey	H. L. Sain	O. A. Warren
	R. P. Waynick		

Second Year Medical Class

COWPER

TOMLINSON

LUPTON

QUICKEL

Second Year Medical Class

R. B. G. COWPER...President
T. H. TOMLINSON..Vice-President
C. C. LUPTON...Secretary-Treasurer
J. C. QUICKEL...Student Councilman

G. C. Allen	G. W. Heinitsh	L. J. Ring
J. M. Andrew	C. F. Hudson	J. M. Robertson
L. A. Andrew	A. A. James	V. B. Rollins
N. O. Bowman	J. R. Johnson	A. S. Rose
L. G. Brown	R. R. Little	C. T. Smith
L. M. Caldwell	R. E. Lore	A. T. Strickland
H. L. Clapp	C. C. Lupton	T. H. Tomlinson
R. B. G. Cowper	D. R. McEachern	T. G. Upchurch
B. B. Dalton	P. R. Maulden	E. N. Walker
J. N. Dawson	W. C. Mebane	N. E. Ward
G. L. Donnelly	J. M. Mewborn	J. B. Westmoreland
G. S. Edgerton	Gladys Morgan	W. E. Wilkinson
C. P. Graham	S. E. Pace	Frank Wilson
	J. C. Quickel	

FIRST YEAR MEDICAL CLASS

KNOEFEL   STONE   HALL

First Year Medical Class

R. E. STONE..President

A. E. KNOEFEL, JR...Vice-President

J. B. HALL...Secretary-Treasurer

J. M. Alexander	C. H. Gay	E. V. Moore	S. W. Vance
L. Appel	W. B. Green	T. McG. Northrop	W. W. Vaughan
A. E. Barnhart	J. B. Hall	R. M. Oliver	W. S. Wall
E. I. Christian	H. C. Harrill	H. M. Price	W. R. Wandeck
M. Dworin	A. N. Johnson	J. T. Ramsaur	S. E. Way
W. H. Flythe	C. M. Kendrick	A. M. Scarborough	P. G. Weil
W. O'K. Fowler	J. W. Kitchen	G. C. Shinn	J. A. Whitaker
H. W. Fox	A. E. Knoefel, Jr.	R. E. Stone	R. W. Wilkins
W. A. Fritz	J. C. McAlister	H. E. Talmadge	R. Winborne, Jr.
R. B. Garrison	L. M. McKee	J. A. Turner, Jr.	B. L. Woodard

MANNING HALL

CALDWELL HALL

ACTIVITIES

William Shakespeare

SHAKESPEARE

What we can do, we'll do, to do you service.

—TIMON OF ATHENS.

COFFIN LEAR

DUNGAN DUNN GALLAND

The Publications Union Board

W. CLYDE DUNN, *President*

J. ELWIN DUNGAN, *Secretary*

J. M. LEAR, *Treasurer*

O. J. COFFIN

HARRY J. GALLAND

ALBRIGHT

GRAHAM

BROWN

DUNN

GALLAND

KINCAID

ATKINSON

HAMER

DAVIS

BOATWRIGHT

TAYLOR

PETTY

The Yackety Yack Editorial Staff

TRAVIS BROWN...*Editor-in-Chief*
ROBERT GRAHAM...*Associate Editor*
HARRY GALLAND...*Associate Editor*
CLYDE DUNN...*Assistant Editor*
MAYNE ALBRIGHT...*Assistant Editor*
HERBERT TAYLOR...*Faculty*
DOUGLAS KINCAID...*Seniors*
ED HAMER...*Other Classes*
HOLMES DAVIS...*Activities*
SWIFT BOATWRIGHT...*Fraternities*
WILLIAM PETTY...*Dance*
BILLY ATKINSON...*Sports*
NICK DOCKERY...*Photography*

Ed Kidd	Jim Kenan	Bert Haywood
Bob Mebane	Joe Adams	George Waterhouse
Charles Allison	Tom Worth	Howard Wilson
Ed Yarborough	Tom Wright	Henry Anderson
Ed Davis	Lawrence Harris	Harry Bunn

The Yackety Yack Business Staff

B. MOORE PARKER...Business Manager

CLAUDE FARRELL ....Assistant Business Manager

HENRY TEMPLE...Collection Manager

June Gunter
Norman Klein
Steve Marsh
Duval Lennon
Clyde Duncan
Sam Silverstein
James Gatlin
Charles Gault
Ben Parker

Tom Johnson
Maurice Eighme
William Hall
Ted Levy
Ed Marshall
Harold Staton
Sherman Shore
J. D. McNairy
Bill White

McNAIRY   HODGES   HOLDER   WILLIAMS   JONES

SHORE   DUNGAN   W. YARBOROUGH   DENNING   RAMSAY

The Daily Tar Heel

GLENN HOLDER..Editor-in-Chief

WILL YARBOROUGH..Managing Editor

Associate Editors

John Mebane   Harry Galland

Assistant Editors

Robert Hodges   J. D. McNairy

Joe Jones   B. C. Moore

J. C. Williams

City Editors

E. F. Yarborough   K. C. Ramsay

Elbert Denning   J. E. Dungan

Sherman Shore

Sports Editor

Henry L. Anderson

Assistant Sports Editors

Brown Roach   J. G. deR. Hamilton, Jr.

HARRIS — MEBANE — ALEXANDER — GALLAND — KARRIKER

YARBOROUGH — ROACH — ANDERSON — HAMILTON — MOORE

Reporters

Holmes Davis	Kemp Yarborough	Nathan Volkman	George Barber
Louis Brooks	Clyde Deitz	W. A. Shulenberger	Henry Wood
Charles Rose	George Seram	G. E. French	Jack Bessen
Mary Price	Frank Manheim	Vass Shepherd	Everard Shemwell
Bill Roberts	B. H. Whitton	B. H. Barnes	Ted Newland
J. P. Tyson	J. M. Little	M. M. Dunlap	Jack Riley
E. C. Daniel	Hugh Wilson	Howard M. Lee	John Patrick

J. J. Dratler

Business Staff

MARION ALEXANDER..*Business Manager*

Ashley Seawell	Bill Speight	Harry Latta
John Jemison	Tom Badger	Donald Seawell

Collection Managers

J. C. Harris	T. R. Karriker
B. C. Prince, Jr.	Stuart Carr

[181]

FARRELL

EDSON

GALLAND

McKEITHAN

WHEARY

DANNENBAUM

GILCHRIST

The Carolina Buccaneer

CY EDSON...*Editor-in-Chief*
GIL PEARSON...*Art Editor*
CRAWFORD MCKETHAN...*Associate Editor*
KERMIT WHEARY..*Associate Editor*
CLAUDE FARRELL..*Assistant Editor*
HARRY GALLAND...*Assistant Editor*
MARY PRICE..*Exchange Editor*
PETE GILCHRIST
GEORGE DANNENBAUM } ....*Managing Editors*

Editorial Staff

Phil Peacock	George Sulkin	Bob Betts
John J. Smith	Amos Hill Taylor	T. P. Tyson
"Doc" Foster		Duval Lennon

Art Staff

Bobbie Mason	Ted Newland	Walter Mason
"Red" Manning	Katherine Noland	Henry Anderson
Jack Sherrill	A. M. Lansford	James Sawyer

I. MANNING   IDOL   PATTERSON   JAMESON   J. MANNING

DAVIS   CLINARD   HARRIS   WILLIAMS

The Carolina Buccaneer

H. N. Patterson _____Business Manager

Harlan Jameson _____Assistant Business Manager

John D. Idol _____Assistant Business Manager

I. H. Manning _____Advertising Manager

James Harris _____Collection Manager

Stuart Carr   Charles Kluttz
John Clinard, Jr.   John Manning
Robert Davis   Richard Marshall
Ed Hamer   F. G. McPherson
James Harris   Alston Watkins
P. C. Idol   J. C. Williams
W. A. Lane   Edgar Thomas

MEBANE CHACE CURTIS

HOLDER DUNLAP ALEXANDER

The Carolina Magazine

JOHN MEBANE..Editor

RICHARD CHACE..Associate Editor

JAY CURTIS..Associate Editor

MARION ALEXANDER..Business Manager

Louis V. Brooks   Glenn Holder
James Dawson   Philip K. Kaufman
J. E. Dungan   J. D. McNairy
Mary Marshall Dunlap   Dorothy Mumford
Milton Greenblatt   J. J. Slade, Jr.
Robert Hodges   J. C. Williams

[184]

FARRIS   PATTERSON   GRAHAM   FUSSELL

WALL   McDANIELS   QUICKEL   BOLEN

The Student Council

R. S. FARRIS .... *President Student Body*

H. N. PATTERSON .... *Secretary Student Council*

R. L. GRAHAM .... *Senior Representative*

L. H. FUSSELL .... *Junior Representative*

E. C. WALL .... *Sophomore Representative*

G. D. McDANIEL .... *Law School Representative*

J. C. QUICKEL .... *Medical School Representative*

H. E. BOLEN .... *Pharmacy School Representative*

THE UNIVERSITY GLEE CLUB

DYER

SCURLOCK

LYNCH   LYON

The University of North Carolina Glee Club

Direction

HAROLD S. DYER..*Director*
NELSON O. KENNEDY.. *Pianist*
E. S. CLARK..*Student Director*

Official Staff

J. P. SCURLOCK.................*President*
T. C. REYNOLDS.............*Vice-President*
S. A. LYNCH, JR......................*Secretary*

Business Staff

H. L. LYON, JR......*Business Manager*
C. B. OVERMAN......*Asst. Business Mgr.*
W. G. BROWN.............................*Librarian*

First Tenor

Charles Aiken	Jay Glenn	S. A. Lynch, Jr.	William Petty	W. T. Whitsett
Charles Duffy	Frank Howell	E. L. Midgett	E. L. Swain	George Winston
		M. P. Park		

Second Tenor

C. H. Ballard	W. L. Boynton	J. P. Hill	T. E. Marshall	J. W. Slaughter
William Barfield	J. C. Connolly	F. M. Laxton, Jr.	H. N. Parsley	Linwood Snell
George Bennett	W. T. Davis	R. F. Lowery	Egbert Peeler	F. P. Spruill
C. E. Best	C. H. Elkins	H. L. Lyon, Jr.	Browning Roach	J. H. Stewart
Gilbert Blauman				F. P. Stompson

First Bass

William Allsbrook	E. V. Conrad	W. F. Humphries	C. B. Overman	Descum Roberts
H. A. Boyd	A. H. Fleming, Jr.	W. L. Hunt	P. R. Patten	Herbert Thomas
T. W. Bremer	L. F. Hammond	Dodd Linker	T. C. Reynolds	G. I. Trull
E. S. Clark	W. R. Hoffman		Pryor Rodwell, Jr.	Earl Williams

Second Bass

R. C. Atwood	J. L. Dickenson	Harland Jameson	Lawrence Ross	M. B. Thomas
Gilles Brown	C. H. Fisher	J. E. Miller	J. P. Scurlock	C. H. Whedbee
Pierre Campbell	Edward Ferguson	F. M. Prouty	A. J. Stahr .	Kenneth Wilson
Paul Carter	J. C. Goodwin		Robert Staton	H. N. Zelley

| EAGLES | WILLIAMS | LANG | HAMER |

The Y. M. C. A. Cabinets

JIMMY WILLIAMS..*President of Y.M.C.A.*

JOHN LANG ....*Vice-President*

JOE EAGLES... *Secretary*

ED HAMER..*Treasurer*

The Junior-Senior Cabinet

Mayne Albright	Carl Fisher	T. R. Karriker	Dave Nims	K. C. Ramsay
Johnson Alexander	Roscoe Fisher	John Lang	A. D. Kincaid	J. B. Schneider
Bill Carbine	Noah Goodridge	I. H. Manning	Frank O'Neil	Huber Taylor
Clyde Dunn	Ed Hamer	Beverly Moore	Pat Patterson	Jimmie Williams
Joe Eagles				J. C. Williams

The Sophomore Cabinet

Henry Anderson	A. N. Daniels	Tom Follin	G. H. Leonard	J. B. Spell
J. D. Barnes	A. E. Douglass	G. E. French	Henry London	H. H. Taylor
Swift Boatwright	W. F. Draper	L. I. Gupton	T. E. Marshall	M. F. Tinkham
Bill Bridgers	Oscar Dressler	W. F. Humphries	C. G. Mock	Craig Wall
E. V. Conrad	L. J. Felton	F. M. James	John Park	S. M. Yancey
J. P. Cooper	Harry Finch	Harlan Jameson	R. C. Pond	Ed Yarborough

The Freshman Friendship Council

Charles Allison	J. E. Cuthrell	C. S. Holshouser	F. T. Phillips	Harold Smith
Bob Atwood	Archie Davis	Bob Hubbard	R. L. Pickett	J. H. Smith
J. M. Auman	Otis Davis	Percy Idol	J. R. Raper	A. M. Steele
Dallie Barham	R. D. Davis	Jimmy Kurfees	Lee Richardson	James Steere
Bob Barnett	W. T. Davis	Joe Lineberger	Raymond Ritchie	John Strickland
Alex Biggs	Bob Drane	George London	W. G. Roberts	F. E. Thomas
Henry Boyd	L. A. Dudley	J. N. McCaskill	C. G. Rose	Nathan Volkman
Charles Brawley	C. S. Forbes	Billy McKee	L. W. Ross	George Vick
J. K. Bridgers	J. E. Fountain	John Manning	S. C. Schenk	Billy Walker
Ben Campen	A. C. Furchgott	Bill Markham	J. A. Sherrill	Alex Webb
A. L. Brooks	Moody Gaither	W. H. Moore	James Shuford	C. S. Weeks
V. L. Brown	R. S. Gidney	Bob Mebane	Vass Shepherd	H. J. Weiland
Pierre Campbell	Frank Ham	Ted Newland	W. C. Singletary	Tom Worth
J. A. Clarke	H. M. Hodges	Nutt Parsley	Louis Skinner	Tom Wright
F. B. Cooper				Billy Walker

THE JUNIOR-SENIOR Y.M.C.A. CABINET

THE SOPHOMORE Y.M.C.A. CABINET

THE FRESHMAN FRIENDSHIP COUNCIL

WELLS   MELLICK   HARDING   McKINNIE   DENT

The Woman's Association

ITTY WELLS ....President

NN MELLICK ....Vice-President

HOEBE HARDING..Secretary

LIVIA McKINNIE...Treasurer

UE DENT...House President

rs. Charlotte G. Adams	Mary A. Carter	Sara G. Falkner
ouise Adams	Olivia H. Chamberlain	Lucine Farmer
ary E. Adams	Ethel May Chapin	Elzada Feaster
lorence E. Ahner	Nellie Rives Cheek	Martha Willson Fenn
enelope B. Alexander	Elizabeth I. Christian	Mary K. Fleming
annie M. Ange	Christine LeR. Coffey	Dorothy Fooshe
ancy Arnold	Eleanor R. Coker	Mrs. Marguerite C. Ford
iriam L. Ashmore	Beth Colley	Maurine Forester
arol A. Ballenger	Georgia A. Couch	Cornelia E. Frizzelle
arolyn R. Banner	Carolyn C. Cox	Marjorie Good .
lizabeth S. Barber	Elsa S. Craig	Julia Graham
elen Louise Baylor	Lillian B. Crisfield	Kate C. Graham
lacid B. Bennett	Helen J. Crosson	Fannie M. Grainger
ora Beust	Anne Kelso Currie	Elizabeth M. Grant
adie M. Bivens	Sydney M. Curry	Mrs. G. P. Grisette
uth Blackwelder	Harriet Lane Daniel	Mrs. Nora D. Gumble
vie M. Bobo	Julia C. Davis	Ruth E. Hamill
ladys A. Boyington	Suzanne T. Dent	Lelia B. Hampton
innie Brashear	Virginia Lyn Denton	Mary K. Harbin
azel L. Brown	Claire J. Douglas	Phoebe Harding
argaret J. Bruton	Virginia A. Douglas	Annie Olivia Harmon
uby D. Buck	Inez S. Dudley	Mrs. Loraine P. Hart
argaret R. Bullitt	Clyde Mason Duncan	Laurine Haynes .
ary Burroughs	Mary Marshall Dunlap	Sarah Frances Heacock
arah J. Bush	Celeste Edgerton	Katherine N. Hendricks
eny Bynum	Nancy B. Eliason	Flora M. Hill
rs. Kate J. Carmichel	Jeanette Ernst	Josephine Hill
arly L. Carpenter	Helen Eubanks	Mary Jane Hill
ora Carpenter	Lida H. Eubanks	Bertha C. Hipp

Mrs. Nelle B. Hobbs
Ethel Hood
Elizabeth W. Howland
Addis C. Huske
Tabitha C. Hutaff
Lillie W. Jackson
Sadie F. Jenkins
Esther Clyde Johnson
Elizabeth Johnston
Edith C. Jones
Elizabeth L. Kenfield
Elizabeth C. Kennedy
Katherine M. Kinard
Mrs. Edna Coates King
Date Parks Kitchen
Edith C. Kyles
Helen F. Lance
Rachel Penn Lane
Rosy Lazarus
Ludie C. Lee
Ida Belle Ledbetter
Pearl Rose S. Lintner
Marion S. Love
Virginia Lumpkin
Adelaide M. McAnally
Marion V. McFetridge
Bettie M. McGee
Mary Margaret McLeod
Helen O. McKay
Olivia McKinne
Ruth McCullough
Mrs. H. L. Macon
Edith H. Mangum
Eleanore Martin

Velma D. Matthews
Anne Melick
Mary Ford Miller
Virginia Mae Milmo
Vera Millsaps
Reeme Moore
Stephanie Moore
Hattie Belle Mooring
Gladys Morgan
Edna E. Morrisette
Dorothy Mumford
Elizabeth Murphy
Ruth Newell
Mary C. Norcross
Martha E. Norburn
Crowell Oliver
Annette M. Osborne
Ruth Page
Mathilde M. Parlett
Blanche Penland
Celeste L. Penny
Florence L. Phillips
Emmie F. Polhill
Martha H. Porter
Mabel A. Powell
Mary W. Price
Elizabeth G. Reed
Mary Adelaide Reed
Mrs. Marie E. Reiss
Mary L. Rigsbee
Dorothy Rose Robinson
Mrs. Bertha May Rogers
Mrs. Carrie H. Schwenning
Sallie E. Scott

Catherine Sherard
Connie E. Smith
Mary Phlegar Smith
Mattie D. Snider
Emily White Stevens
Martha Louise Thacker
Mrs. Emma S. Trabue
M. L. Troutman
Lucile Turner
Virginia R. Turner
Henrietta Underwood
Gertrude Vaile
Minnie L. Waldrop
Mary Louise Wall
Mildred Walker
E. Noel Walker
Jessie S. Ward
M. Rebecca Ward
Sarah Elizabeth Ward
Mary Watters
Evelyn Way
Ida Vivian Weaver
Maude M. Webster
Katherine Platt Wells
L. Elaine Wheaton
George Wilcox
Grace A. Williams
Mrs. Helen V. Williams
Lena Mae Williams
Ruth E. Williams
Janet H. Wilson
Mrs. J. C. Wilson
Mary L. Withers
Jewell Louise Yow

American Institute of Electrical Engineers

J. J. ALEXANDER .... President
T. V. HEDGPETH .... Vice-President
F. R. TOMS .... Secretary
W. B. WHITE .... Treasurer

Freshmen

H. M. Allen	T. L. Cordle	W. H. Griffin	G. W. Miller	T. H. Walker
H. M. Barry	C. F. Crum	C. N. Harris	W. J. O'Brien, Jr.	G. H. Ware
F. S. Black	F. G. Dellinger	W. E. Harris	B. C. Proctor	G. O. Weis
A. J. Bost	T. C. Evans	D. R. Hinkle	J. E. Slater	G. C. Worsley
C. L. Bradley	H. S. Fulcher	L. L. Johnson	J. F. Strickland	G. M. Young
J. K. Bridgers	J. K. Galloway	M. M. Jones	J. B. Thompson	H. N. Zelley
H. F. Click	G. W. Gorham	F. H. Justus	A. H. Taylor	J. R. Hubbard
		J. R. Marvin		

Sophomores

G. H. Alford	T. A. Baroody	J. M. Duls	F. M. Glover, Jr.	J. L. Sherrill
H. P. Baldwin	W. D. Bryan	A. H. Eliasson	E. T. Gross	E. L. Swain
S. A. Barham	G. H. Coats, Jr.	E. F. Frisby	C. A. Hensley	D. J. Thurston
		J. L. Fisher		

Juniors

J. T. Boysworth	E. G. Hoefer, Jr.	R. E. Hubbard	W. P. McPherson	A. M. Perez
Page Choate	G. F. Horney	P. G. Johnson, Jr.	W. R. Mills	A. C. Robertson
W. S. Crawford, Jr.	J. M. Houston	O. J. McCall	E. S. Oakes	G. D. Thompson
C. P. Hayes, Jr.				R. V. Whitener

Seniors

J. J. Alexander	F. E. Drake	C. M. Lear	J. E. Sherwood	L. E. Tulloch
W. C. Burnett	T. V. Hedgpeth	D. A. Nims	J. E. Skinner	W. B. White
E. R. Davis	F. B. Kuykendal		F. R. Toms	W. J. Wortman

American Society of Civil Engineers

John Andrews	J. L. Ferebee	J. I. Palmore
R. B. Armfield	P. L. Gilbert	G. N. Pierce
C. H. Atkins	R. W. Goebel	G. J. Quinn
W. M. Atkinson, Jr.	I. A. Groom	A. E. Reynolds
A. T. Allen, Jr.	H. O. Hill	T. M. Riddick
J. F. Barret	W. J. Horney	F. C. Rankin
C. H. Boyd	W. L. Harper	O. D. Stinson
A. C. Brown	C. C. Howard	J. P. Scurlock
W. E. Bobbitt	W. L. Keller	W. O. Southerland
J. L. Brown, Jr.	O. W. Kochtizky	H. P. Thomas
N. L. Bryan	B. B. Lane	C. H. White
M. R. Cowper	E. G. Long	B. Whitton
C. S. Dickie	C. M. Ledbetter	C. E. Waddell
F. G. Dogget	E. P. McLean	R. M. Walford
J. W. Doughtie	H. S. McIver	C. H. West
C. R. Davis	W. M. McKinney	J. G. Wadsworth
A. N. Daniels	A. Mitchel	G. T. Winston
S. J. Dunavant	J. A. Moore	R. J. White
H. T. Erwin	R. H. Moore	W. E. Underhill
	J. L. Norris	

American Society of Mechanical Engineers

E. L. LOWERY.. *President*
R. A. PARSLEY.. *First Vice-President*
J. S. NEWSOM.. *Second Vice-President*
E. L. MIDGETT.. *Secretary*
J. B. PITTANA.. *Treasurer*

Faculty Members

E. G. HOEFER, *Honorary Chairman*   N. P. BAILEY

Student Members

Attilio E. Bevacqua	S. W. Hinson	E. D. Lennon
R. T. Burnett	E. L. Kendrick	J. H. Margolis
Robert Cowhig	Bloomfield Kendall	J. A. McLean
C. C. Cornwall	V. L. Kenyon, Jr.	R. E. Orbaugh
A. W. Dunbar	Frederick Knoop, Jr.	C. L. Petree
A. C. Furgott, Jr.	H. H. Kyle	R. C. Plummer
D. A. Harrell		J. H. Smith

WILLIAMS

WILKINSON

SPEIGHT

HARRIS

ALBRIGHT

The Debate Council

THE Debate Council is the body selected to manage all student inter-collegiate contests of a forensic nature—oratory and debating—engaged in by the University. Beginning with the scholastic year 1927-28, with the consent of the University Administration, the two Literary Societies, and the Student Body, the Debate Council was organized in its present form, which is essentially as follows: It is composed of four students and three faculty members—two of the student members are appointed by the President of the University. The President of the Debate Council is always a student, and one of the faculty members is always Executive Secretary, the latter office continuing from year to year.

The present composition of the Debate Council is as follows: J. C. Williams, President; Professor George M. McKie, Executive Secretary; Professor Howard M. Jones, Professor Frank P. Graham, R. M. Albright, J. A. Wilkinson, J. C. Harris, and W. W. Speight.

THE DIALECTIC SENATE

WILLIAMS

McPHERSON

RECTOR

The Dialectic Senate

J. C. WILLIAMS..President, Fall Term
GARLAND MCPHERSON..President, Winter Term
T. B. RECTOR...President, Spring Term

Members

Adams, W. J., Jr.	Farris, R. S.	Parsley, R. A.	Whitmire, T. C.	Ramsay, K. C.
Armstrong, D. H.	Follin, Marion	Parham, J. M.	Wimbish, Paul	Parker, B. M.
Alexander, J. M.	Griggs, C. F.	Patterson, H. N.	Yarborough, W. H.	Barnett, R. W.
Armfield, John	Goodson, C. F.	Royster, C. L.	Wright, G. R.	Adams, J. B.
Burch, F. B., Jr.	Greene, R. S.	Rector, Beatty	Hines, G. N.	Snider, A.
Brooks, C. M.	Gray, R. M.	Simpson, M. B.	Wilson, G. W.	Kenan, J. G.
Bliss, W. M.	Galland, H. J.	Shedd, W. B.	Starbuck, W. W.	Rose, C. G.
Bissell, W. N.	Hamer, E. R.	Sherfessee, Louis, Jr.	Lamm, R. W.	Yarborough, K.
Blond, C. A. Jr.	Henderson, W. J.	Sechler, C. W.	Moore, M. P.	Brooks, A. L., Jr.
Bunett, W. C.	Hunter, E. C.	Seawell, M. B.	McKee, W. W.	Shepherd, W. V.
Cates, C. C.	Kincaid, G. A.	Tatum, C. C.	Wardlaw, Jack	Hammond, L. T.
Covington, R. O.	Karriker, T. R.	Torbert, J. F.	Herkimer, B. J.	Patterson, F. G.
Coggins, G. R.	Little, A. D.	Thomas, F. A.	Jackson, S. D.	Maybank, G. W.
Dunn, Clyde	Morgan, R. H.	Williams, J. R.	Van Cleave, P.	Phillips, C. T.
Davis, G. T.	Marshall, B. A.	White, W. W.	Parsley, H. N.	Dickenson, J. L.
Davis, W. G.	McMichael, J. M.	Webb, R. H.	Webb, A.	Wright, L. C.
Douglas, A. E.	McCandless, John	Williams, J. C.	Dickson, T. S.	Wright, T. W.
Dockery, N. W.	McIver, C. R.	Whisnant, H. P.	Meadford, W. C.	McCorkle, W. C.
—Dungan, J. E.	McPherson, Garland	Whitsett, W. T.	Shreve, C. A.	Wood, H.
English, D. L.	Moore, B. C.	Williams, J. S.	Little, J. M.	Williams, J. R., Jr.
Edson, C. M.	Moore, J. O., Jr.	Wardlaw, C. D.	Dratler, J. J.	Flinn, L.
French, G. E.	Newman, G. F.	Wardlaw, F. C.	Conrad, E.	Fleming-Jones, R. M.

THE PHILANTHROPIC ASSEMBLY

SPEIGHT

LANG

CARR

The Philanthropic Society

W. W. SPEIGHT..*Speaker, Fall Term*
J. A. LANG ....*Speaker, Winter Term*
G. P. CARR ....*Speaker, Spring Term*

R. M. Albright
Robert Atwood
J. M. Auman
M. E. Aycocke
T. R. Baldwin
A. T. Barnes
H. M. Barnes
T. B. Beckham
W. W. Blackman
V. L. Brown
C. W. Carleton
G. P. Carr
T. B. Campen
D. H. Clifton
W. T. Crutchfield
Clarence Davis
J. R. Denning
C. C. Duffy
E. B. Ferguson
R. A. Ferguson
L. J. Felton
C. S. Forbes

Lee Greer
B. L. Haywood
J. F. Hester
J. R. Horne
H. H. Hobgood
R. D. Huff
T. W. Hughes
C. C. Jackson
H. T. Jackson
J. F. Jackson
F. M. James
A. D. Kornegay
J. A. Lang
H. M. Lee
P. G. Lee
D. C. McDuffie
W. S. Montgomery
Alfredo Nazerino
E. A. Neely
M. Outlaw
J. G. Pleasant
R. W. Poole

Charles Powell
J. H. Pratt
C. A. Renn
B. E. Strickland
W. W. Speight
J. B. Spell
Walter Stone
R. E. Stanton
H. T. Taylor
W. E. Uzzell
J. W. Vann
Herman Vinson
J. E. Wall
G. B. Weaver
C. H. Whedbee
W. R. Whittington
J. A. Wilkinson
N. B. Woodard
T. C. Worth
E. F. Yarborough
T. T. Zoeflor
J. G. Zaglin

WILLIAMS

HARRIS

STANTON

The Mary D. Wright Debate

December 10, 1929

THE Mary D. Wright Memorial Medal was begun years ago by the late P. E. Wright, of Landis, N. C., and is now continued by his estate through the agency of the present Mr. P. E. Wright, of the same place. It is awarded to the better speaker of the winning team in the annual December debate between the Dialectic Senate and the Philanthropic Assembly.

The debate for the scholastic year 1929-30 was on the query: "Resolved, That the Smoot-Hawley bill now pending before the special session of the seventy-first congress should be passed as introduced."

The representatives of the Philanthropic Assembly were J. C. Harris and R. E. Stanton. They upheld the affirmative. The Dialectic Senate's negative aggregation was composed of C. A. Shreve and J. C. Williams.

The Mary D. Wright Memorial Medal was won by J. C. Williams, of the Dialectic Senate.

CARR

WHITLEY

McPHERSON

WILLIAMS

Bingham Memorial Debate

June 8, 1929

THE Bingham Memorial Debate was begun in 1899 at the instigation of the late Colonel Bingham. The Bingham medal is now given annually by Mr. R. W. Bingham in honor of his distinguished ancestor. The debate is always held during commencement, the medal being awarded to the best speaker of the contest. The contestants are representatives of the two campus literary societies.

The debate for the scholastic year 1928-29 was on the query: "Resolved, That the United States should join the World Court."

The representatives of the Dialectic Senate were J. C. Williams and F. G. McPherson. They upheld the affirmative side. The Philanthropic Assembly was represented by G. P. Carr and E. H. Whitley on the negative side of the issue. The affirmative was declared winner.

The Bingham Memorial Medal was awarded to J. C. Williams, of the Dialectic Senate.

WILLIAMS   WHITLEY

Debate Between the University of North Carolina and the University of Kentucky

March 4, 5, 6, 7, 1929

QUERY: *"Resolved,* That the public should own and operate the hydro-electric power plants of the country, with the exception of those which are already under private control and ownership."

ON the above dates the representatives of the University of North Carolina, J. C. Williams, '30' and E. H. Whitley, '30' debated the representatives of the University of Kentucky at various points in the State of Kentucky—the final debate being held in the University auditorium, Lexington. This series of debates on the question of hydro-electric power was designed to be an educational program, since this matter was expected to constitute a major issue in the next gubernatorial campaign in Kentucky.

The representatives of the University of North Carolina upheld the affirmative side of the question. All of the debates were no-decision discussions.

FISHER   HAYWOOD

Debate Between the University of North Carolina
and the University of Texas

March 5, 1929

QUERY: *"Resolved,* That the United States should join
the World Court without reservations."

THIS debate was held at Chapel Hill as a special feature of the celebration conducted by the Texas Club of the University of North Carolina in commemoration of the independence of Texas. R. B. Fisher, '31' and E. L. Haywood, '31' representing the University of North Carolina, upheld the negative side of the question. The Texas team won an audience decision.

BROWN

BLEDSOE

HOBGOOD

Debate Between the University of North Carolina and Harvard University

April 9, 1929

QUERY: *"Resolved,* That loyalty is the ·curse of the American College."

THIS debate was held at Chapel Hill, the University of North Carolina taking the negative side of the question, and being represented by L. T. Bledsoe, Law; H. N. Brown, III, '29; and H. H. Hobgood, '32· The debate was ·a no-decision contest.

SPEIGHT   WILLIAMS

Radio Debate Between the University of North Carolina and the University of Virginia

April 25, 1929

QUERY: *"Resolved,* That national advertising as it is
now practiced is both socially and economically
harmful."

THIS, the first radio debate in which the University of North Carolina ever
participated, was broadcast from Station WRVA, Richmond. J. C. Williams,
'30' and W. W. Speight, '30' representing the University of North Carolina, upheld
the affirmative side of the controversy.

CARR

HOBGOOD

MASHBURN

Triangular Debate Between the University of North Carolina, Wake Forest College, and N. C. State College

December 12, 1929

QUERY: *"Resolved,* That the nations of the world should adopt some plan of complete disarmament, excepting such forces as are needed for police purposes."

IN the Carolina-Wake Forest end of this debate, at Chapel Hill, G. P. Carr, '30, and T. E. Denton, '33, won a unanimous decision. The representatives of the University upheld the affirmative side of the question. The Carolina negative team of H. H. Hobgood, '32, and T. M. Mashburn, '33, upheld the negative side of the issue in a no-decision debate against N. C. State College at Raleigh.

BALEY   MEARES

Debate Between the University of North Carolina
and the University of South Carolina

December 13, 1929

QUERY: *"Resolved,* That the nations of the world should adopt some plan of complete disarmament, excepting such forces as are needed for police purposes."

THIS debate was held at Columbia, S. C., the University of North Carolina taking the negative side of the controversy, and being represented by J. M. Baley, '31, and C. W. Meares, '31· The South Carolina team won the decision.

CARR   FISHER

Debate Between the University of North Carolina and Emory University

QUERY: *"Resolved,* That the United States should join
the World Court without reservations."

G. P. Carr, '30, and R. B. Fisher, '31, were selected to represent the University of North Carolina in a debate against Emory University, at Atlanta. Emory, however, cancelled the debate a few days before it was scheduled to occur.

WILKINSON

SPEIGHT

WILLIAMS

Debates Between the University of North Carolina, Emory University, and Georgia School of Technology

February 26 and 27, 1930

QUERY: *"Resolved,* That modern science tends to destroy theistic faith."

THESE debates were held at Atlanta, the University of North Carolina taking the affirmative side of the question in both of them, and being represented against Emory by W. W. Speight, '30, and McB. Fleming-Jones, '31; and being represented against Georgia Tech. by J. C. Williams, '30, and J. A. Wilkinson, '31.

CARR

BALEY·

MEARES   HOBGOOD

Debates Between the University of North Carolina
and George Washington University

February 28 and March 2

QUERY: *"Resolved,* That the nations of the world
should adopt some plan of complete disarmament, excepting such forces as are needed for
police purposes."

UPHOLDING the affirmative side of the question, the University of North
Carolina team, composed of G. P. Carr, '30, and J. M. Baley, '31, met the
representatives of George Washington University, at Chapel Hill, on February 28.
On March 2, H. H. Hobgood, '32, and C. W. Meares, '31, upheld the negative end
of the question against the George Washington debaters at Washington.

KALEIDOSCOPE

O. Henry

O. HENRY

For the shifting scenery of this globe of ours requires close attention.

—THE TRIMMED LAMP.

THAT FAR-FAMED WELL

ACROSS TO SOUTH

UNDER THE BLANKET

SUNLIGHT
AND
SHADOW

FROM SAUNDERS
EAST

SHOWING HER
PETTICOATS

IN MEMORIAM

ACTION AGAINST
VIRGINIA

WITH THE BIG
BASS DRUM

HALF

VOX POPULI

BRANCH-AND THE SCORE 14-O

VARSITY FENCERS

PARRY & REPOSTE

VARSITY TENNIS COURTS

THE
GREAT
INDOORS

INDOOR CHAMPIONSHIP MEET

REFRIGERATING CROSS COUNTRY

RUBLE FLIES HIGH

THE BEST SHOW IN TOWN

HORSES-HORSES

SATURDAY AFTERNOON CROWD

WIDE AWAKE TAR HEEL STAFF

BROADWAY FROM THE TRAFFIC TOWER

FALSE ALARM

HAVE A CIGAR?

FRATERNITIES
AND
SOCIAL ORDERS

Lord Chesterfield

LORD CHESTERFIELD

To keep good company, especially at your first setting out, is to receive a good impression of the world.
—LETTERS TO HIS SON.

INTERFRATERNITY COUNCIL

BULLUCK, PRES.
ΣΚ

WILLIAMS, SEC'Y.
ΠΚΦ

CHATHAM
ΔΚΕ

BROWN
ΦΓΔ

RACE
ΒΘΠ

GAY
ΔΥ

SWOPE
ΧΨ

NIMS
ΦΚΣ

HOLMES
ΣΑΕ

ALBRIGHT
ΖΨ

HAYWOOD
ΧΦ

ERICKSON
ΑΤΩ

WARD
ΚΑ

DALEY
ΦΔΘ

HAMER
ΣΝ

BAGBY
ΚΣ

MOODY
ΠΚΑ

MERRITT
ΔΣΦ

ALEXANDER
ΘΧ

JACKSON
ΔΤΔ

SAPP
ΣΦΕ

FELSHIN
ΤΕΦ

TAYLOR
ΘΚΝ

TAYLOR
ΑΛΤ

WALKER
ΛΧΑ

FORD
ΣΦΣ

JONES
ΦΣΚ

GALLAND
ΖΒΤ

COVINGTON
ΣΖ

BRICK
ΦΑ

[217]

ALEXANDER   BARTLETT   BROOKS   CARMICHAEL   CHATHAM

D.J.CRAIG   J.T.CRAIG   DAVIS   DORTCH   F.H.DUNN

W.DUNN   FENNER   GRAY   HOLDERNESS   KINCAID

KOENIG   LINDLEY   LINEBERGER   MEBANE   NEWCOMBE

SHEPHERD   SMATHERS   WALKER   WATKINS   WILLIS

DELTA KAPPA EPSILON

Founded at Yale, 1844

Colors: Crimson, Blue and Gold   *Publication*: D. K. E. Quarterly

Beta Chapter

Established 1851

Fratres in Facultate

Dr. W. M. Dey   Dr. F. P. Venable

Fratres in Universitate

Class of 1930

David J. Craig, Jr.   Gordon Gray
Julian B. Fenner   Haywood D. Holderness
William S. Koenig

Class of 1931

Robert V. Brawley   Charles G. Chatham
John T. Craig   Gavin H. Dortch
William Dunn   Archibald D. Kincaid, Jr.
John V. Lindley   Alston S. Watkins
Claude L. Whichard   Meade H. Willis

Class of 1932

Thomas W. Alexander   George L. Barlett
Frank H. Dunn   John W. McAllister
Thomas L. Parsons   Frank Smathers, Jr.
Mandeville A. Webb

Law

John B. McMullen   Horatio N. Woodson

Pledges

Aubrey L. Brooks, Jr.   Robert H. Carmichael
Raymond H. Chatham   Archibald K. Davis
Joseph W. Lineberger   Robert J. Mebane, Jr.
Elliot H. Newcombe   John A. Preston
William V. Shepherd   Edwin G. Walker

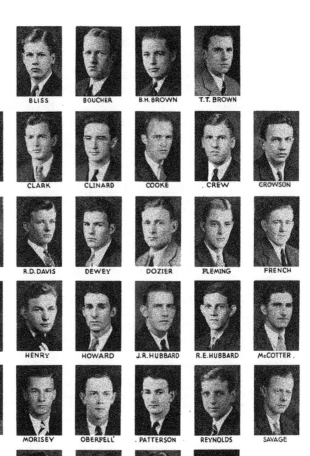

BLISS   BOUCHER   B.H. BROWN   T.T. BROWN

BRYAN   CLARK   CLINARD   COOKE   CREW   CROWSON

F. P. DAVIS   R. D. DAVIS   DEWEY   DOZIER   FLEMING   FRENCH

GRAHAM   HENRY   HOWARD   J.R. HUBBARD   R.E. HUBBARD   McCOTTER

McLEOD   MORISEY   OBERFELL   PATTERSON   REYNOLDS   SAVAGE

C.W. TAYLOR   H.H. TAYLOR   WHITE   YOUNG

PHI GAMMA DELTA
Founded at Washington and Jefferson College, 1848

Color: Royal Purple   *Flower*: Purple Clematis

Publication: The Phi Gamma Delta

Epsilon Chapter·
Established 1851

Fratres in Facultate
ERNEST L. MACKIE, PH.D.   JAMES B. BULLITT, M.D.
STERLING A. STOUDEMIRE, M.A.

Fratre in Urbe
LUTHER J. PHIPPS

Fratres in Universitate
Class of 1930 ·
BERTRAM H. BROWN   ROBERT L. GRAHAM
DeWITT C. McCOTTER

Class of 1931
STANLEY E. CREW   ROBERT E. HUBBARD
KENT CRUESER   HENRY N. PATTERSON
ROBERT F. DEWEY   ARTHUR E. REYNOLDS
BERRY G. FRENCH   CHALMERS L. WHITE, JR.

Class of 1932
WILLIAM M. BLISS   DONALD P. COOKE
WILLIAM D. BRYAN, JR.   CHARLES E. TAYLOR
STUART L. CLARK   CHARLES W. TAYLOR
JOHN W. CLINARD, JR.   HERBERT H. TAYLOR, JR.

Law
TRAVIS T. BROWN

Pledges
GEORGE P. BOUCHER   CHAMP C. HENRY
ROBERT B. BROCK   WILLIAM A. HOWARD
CHARLES A. CROWSON   JAMES R. HUBBARD
FRANK P. DAVIS   FRANK A. McLEOD
ROBERT D. DAVIS   JACK C. MORISEY
JOHN S. DOZIER   GILBERT F. OBERFELL
ARTHUR H. FLEMING   FRANCIS L. SAVAGE
GROSSER M. YOUNG

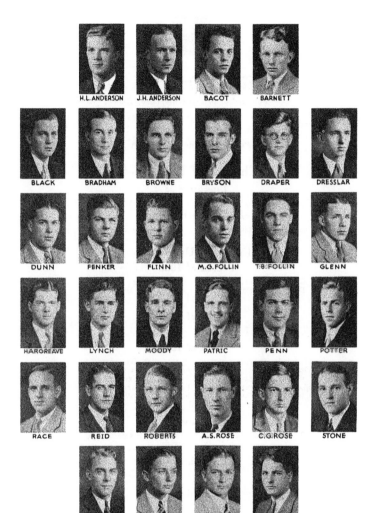

H.L. ANDERSON J.H. ANDERSON BACOT BARNETT

BLACK BRADHAM BROWNE BRYSON DRAPER DRESSLAR

DUNN FENKER FLINN M.G. FOLLIN T.B. FOLLIN GLENN

HARGREAVE LYNCH MOODY PATRIC PENN POTTER

RACE REID ROBERTS A.S. ROSE C.G. ROSE STONE

WADDELL C.D. WARDLAW F.C. WARDLAW WILSON

BETA THETA PI
Founded at Miami University, 1839

Colors: Pink and Blue   *Flower:* Rose

Publication: Beta Theta Pi

Eta Chapter of Beta Theta Pi
Established 1852

Fratres in Facultate
ALVIN S. WHEELER, PH.D.   KENT J. BROWN, PH.D.

Fratres in Universitate

Class of 1930
GEORGE W. BRADHAM   GEORGE RACE
DOUGLAS L. POTTER   CHARLES E. WADDELL, JR.
          MARION G. FOLLIN, JR.

Class of 1931
HERBERT T. BROWNE   GEORGE D. MOODY

Class of 1932
HENRY L. ANDERSON   WILLIAM F. DRAPER
OSCAR W. DRESSLAR   FRANK H. CHAMBERLAIN, JR.
THOMAS B. FOLLIN   RICHARD M. FENKER
MARION S. GLENN   FRANK L. SAMPLE, JR.
CHARLES D. WARDLAW, JR.   FREDERICK C. WARDLAW
          DONALD B. WAUGH

Law
T. A. UZZELL, JR.   JOHN H. ANDERSON, JR.
          P. W. GLIDEWELL

Medicine
AUGUSTUS S. ROSE

Pledges
ROBERT W. BARNETT   WILLIAM G. ROBERTS   JAMES M. LYNCH
FISHER S. BLACK   GEORGE G. STONE   JOHN PATRIC
JOSEPH E. DUNN   WALTER W. BACOT   GARRISON REID
ANDREW HARGREAVE   HOLMES BRYSON, JR.   CHARLES G. ROSE, JR.
JOSEPH J. McGAULEY   LAWRENCE FLINN   J. RUSSELL WILLIAMS, JR.
C. ASHBY PENN, JR.   WILLIAM T. WILSON

BRANDT   BYERLY   CARTER   CASE

FISHER   GAY   GRAINGER   HAINES

KEIM   KESLER   LEA   PADDISON

PAXTON   ROGERS   SCHNELL   TIMBERLAKE

DELTA PSI
Founded at Columbia University, 1847

St. Anthony Hall of University of North Carolina
Established 1854

Fratres in Universitate
Class of 1930
JOHN BRANDT   HERMAN WALKER SCHNELL

Class of 1931
CHARLES ROBERT ERSKINE   ADAM FISHER, JR.
KENNETH ALEXANDER GAY   JOHN CAMERON GRAINGER
            BRANCHE EDWARDS PAXTON

Class of 1932
WALLACE TALMADGE CASE   SYDNEY LONGSTRETH W. LEA
ALFRED HOWARD PADDISON   GEORGE CLIFTON KEIM
            STEPHEN DAVIS TIMBERLAKE, III

Law
FREDERICK LEE BYERLY

Graduate
ROLAND LINCOLN KESLER

Pledges
PAUL STUART CARTER   HAROLD ATLA HAINES, JR.
            CARROLL PICKENS ROGERS, JR.

ATWOOD   AVERY   BAGGS

BENNETT   BLAIR   COWHIG   DAY

GLASCOCK   HOVIS   MITCHAM   NORMAN

REEVES   SWOPE   WHITE   WALLACE

CHI PSI

Founded at Union College, 1841

Colors: Purple and Gold   *Publication*: The Purple and Gold

Alpha Sigma Chapter

Established 1855

Fratres in Facultate

W. D. Toy   R. E. Coker
W. C. Coker   G. C. Taylor
A. R. Hollett

Fratres in Universitate

Class of 1930

Henry McK. Baggs   Robert A. Hovis
William O. Bennett   Granville H. Swope

Class of 1931

W. Kennett Blair   Harold W. Glascock, II
William F. Day   William H. Norman
Roy W. Franklin   Robert Reeves

Class of 1932

Robert H. Avery   Franklin Gray
Thomas Badger, III   Fred B. Greer
Whitner N. Bissell   T. Gilbert Pearson, Jr.
R. E. Coker, Jr.   George N. Pierce, II
John S. White, Jr.

Law

W. S. Malone   G. E. Levings, Jr.
L. W. Wallace   Killian Barwick

Graduate

Burnham S. Colburn, Jr.

Pledges

Charles W. Allison, Jr.   Ellis Dudley
Robert C. Atwood   John F. Jeffreys, Jr.
Pierre Campbell   William C. Mitcham, Jr.
Robert K. Cowhig   William B. McLean
Hubert D. Crow   Joseph H. Norman, III
Thomas A. Davidson   W. Marvin Robey, Jr.
J. Banks Young

ADAMS

BRICKMAN

BROWN

BURWELL

DRANE

KAUFMAN

A.M.KIRKPATRICK

J.J.KIRKPATRICK

J.H.MANNING

J.T.MANNING

MARKHAM

NIMS

RUEHL

SPRUILL

STEERE

TURNER

WALSER

WARDLAW

WHITTON

G.W.WILSON

H.M.WILSON

WINSTON

PHI KAPPA SIGMA

Founded at the University of Pennsylvania, 1850

Colors: Old Gold and Black   *Publication*: Phi Kappa Sigma News Letter

Lambda Chapter of Phi Kappa Sigma
Established 1856

Fratres in Facultate

Isaac H. Manning, M.D.   English Bagby, Ph.D.
Henry H. Williams, Ph.D.   J. Merritt Lear, M.A.
Gregory L. Paine, Ph.D.   Robert H. Sherrill, M.A.
Samuel Selden, B.A.

Fratres in Universitate

Class of 1930

William J. Adams, Jr.   David A. Nims
William L. Hunt   John W. Wardlaw

Class of 1931

Frederick M. Brickman, Jr.   William D. Merritt, Jr.
Arthur M. Kirkpatrick   Michael Schenck, Jr.
John J. Kirkpatrick   Frank P. Spruill, Jr.
Isaac H. Manning, Jr.   George Taylor Winston
E. George Hoefer, Jr.

Class of 1932

W. Gilles Brown   Arthur W. Kaufmann
Richard G. Burwell   Victor E. Ruehl, Jr.
Harry Latta, Jr.   Fredrick M. Prouty
Beaumert H. Whitton

Medicine

James A. Turner, Jr.

Graduate

Richard G. Walser

Pledges

Robert W. Drane   James B. Thompson
John T. Manning   Thomas H. Walker
William S. Markham, Jr.   George W. Wilson, Jr.
James E. Steere, Jr.   Hugh McL. Wilson
John F. Wright

ATKINSON   BOATWRIGHT   BROWN   CARPENTER

CHEATHAM   CONSTANTINE   DAVIS   DUNAVANT   FARLEIGH

GOODRIDGE   HARRIS   HOLMES   HUDSON   HUGER   JEMISON

J.H. LONDON   L.F. LONDON   PARSLEY   RHETT   RUFFIN   SANDERS

SHANNON   SPAULDING   THOMPSON   WATERHOUSE   WEBB

WILY   WOOD   WORTH   E.F.YARBOROUGH   W.H.YARBOROUGH

SIGMA ALPHA EPSILON

Founded at the University of Alabama, 1856

Colors: Old Gold and Purple *Flower:* Violet

Publications: The Record, and Phi Alpha (Secret)

Xi Chapter

Established 1857

Fratres in Facultate

ROBERT D. W. CONNOR, PH.B. EDWARD V. HOWELL, PH.G. W. W. PIERSON, JR., PH.D

ALMONTE C. HOWELL, PH.D. ROBERT H. WETTACH, S.J.D. JAMES N. ASHMORE

GEORGE F. HORNER, A.M. CHARLES MORRIS

Fratres in Universitate

Class of 1930

WILLIAM C. CHEATHAM	ROBERT HOKE WEBB	J. FLEMING WILY, JR.
STUART A. FARLEIGH	GEORGE W. SANDERS	LEON A. SPAULDING

Class of 1931

CUNNINGHAM W. CONSTANTINE	JOHN S. JEMISON	ALBERT M. RHETT
NOAH GOODRIDGE	JOHN H. LONDON	PETER B. RUFFIN
W. W. HEFFELFINGER, JR.	LAWRENCE F. LONDON	WILLIAM C. THOMPSON
JAMES H. HUDSON	E. S. NASH, JR.	EDWARD J. WOOD
W. B. HUGER	R. A. PARSLEY	HAL V. WORTH
	WILLIAM H. YARBOROUGH	

Class of 1932

WILLIAM M. ATKINSON	JOSEPH CARPENTER	LAWRENCE R. HARRIS
SWIFT M. BOATWRIGHT	J. HOLMES DAVIS, JR.	GEORGE WATERHOUSE
ROYALL R. BROWN	JACKSON DUNAVANT	E. F. YARBOROUGH

Law

JUNIUS G. ADAMS	WILLIAM P. FULLER
A. BARON HOLMES	C. J. SHANNON, III

Medicine

FREDERICK W. DICK

Graduates

THOMAS BENNETT MARSDEN BELLAMY, JR.

Pledges

JOEL B. ADAMS	BRYAN GRANT	H. N. PARSLEY
F. G. BALLENGER	I. W. HUGHES	F. G. PATTERSON
W. E. BARNES	J. G. KENAN	ALEXANDER WEBB, JR.
H. G. CONNOR, III	THEODORE MAYBANK	T. C. WORTH
R. L. COVINGTON	W. J. O'BRIEN, JR.	KEMP YARBOROUGH

ALBRIGHT   BAKER   BARBER   CALHOUN

COOPER   A.W. COWPER   M.R. COWPER   R.B.G. COWPER   GILCHRIST

GRAHAM   GREGORY   LYON   McCONNELL   McPHERSON

O'DONNELL   RIDDICK   ROUSE   C.L.SMITH   J.G.SMITH

SNOW   TILLERY   THOMPSON   VALK   WEBB

WILDER   WILLIAMS   B.U.WHITEHEAD   L.W.WHITEHEAD   ZEALY

ZETA PSI

Founded at New York University, 1846

Color: White   Flower: White Carnation

Publication: The Circle

Upsilon Chapter

Established 1858

Fratres in Facultate

EDWARD T. BROWN, M.A.   HENRY JOHNSTON, A.B.   THOMAS J. WILSON, JR., PH.D.
GEORGE HOWE, PH.D.   CHARLES S. MANGUM, M.D.   ROBERT MEADE, A.B.

Fratres in Urbe

LOUIS GRAVES   ROBERT W. WINSTON

Fratres in Universitate

Class of 1930

CHARLES F. WILLIAMS   HOMER LEGRAND LYON, JR.   JOHN W. GRAHAM
NEWTON S. CALHOUN, JR.   CHARLES L. SMITH, JR.   ROBERT ZEALY

Class of 1931

MAYNE ALBRIGHT, JR.   WILLIAM B. SNOW, JR.
WILLIAM P. MCPHERSON   GEORGE D. THOMPSON
BURGESS U. WHITEHEAD   THOMAS M. RIDDICK
WILLIAMS COOPER   MARION R. COWPER

Class of 1932

ALBERT W. COWPER   WOODWARD L. BOYNTON   PETER S. GILCHRIST, JR.
LYNN WILDER   T. NORFLEET WEBB, JR.   EDWARD K. GRAHAM
PAUL A. TILLERY   H. HAYWOOD O'DONNELL   SAMUEL MCCONNELL, JR.
                     HERBERT THORPE GREGORY

Law

CHARLES R. ROUSE   GEORGE V. COWPER, JR.   CHARLES O'H. GRIMES
CHARLES S. MANGUM, JR. THOMAS GOLD   MARVIN WILSON

Medicine

ROSCOE B. GRAY COWPER

Pledges

MILTON A. BARBER   ARTHUR DET. VALK
FREDERICK P. LAXTON   JULIAN T. BAKER
ASHBY L. BAKER   JOSEPH H. PRATT
LOUIS WHITEHEAD   JOHN SMITH

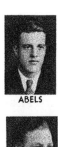  

ABELS   BENOIT   COURSEY

EDSON   ESKEW   C. FARRELL   R. FARRELL   HAYWOOD

HUSKE   KING   LENNON   MacKETHAN   PARRISH

PEELER   PESCHAU   RANDELL   RICHARDSON   SLUSSER

TAYLOR   UPSHAW   WITHERS

CHI PHI

Founded at the College of New Jersey, 1824

Colors: Scarlet and Blue   *Publication*: The Chakett

Alpha Alpha Chapter
Established 1858

Fratres in Urbe
JOSEPH MARYON SAUNDERS   JOHN McIVER FOUSHEE

Fratre in Facultate
GEORGE F. SENSABAUGH

Fratres in Universitate
Class of 1930
BAXTER T. DAVIES   ISAAC HALL HUSKE
CYRUS MELVIN EDSON   LUTHER CORWIN STEWARD
WALTER EUGENE ESKEW.   RALPH L. RANDELL

Class of 1931
JACK BARROWS COURSEY   ERNEST DUVAL LENNON
ROBERT FARRELL   CRAWFORD BIGGS MACKETHAN
CLAUDE FARRELL   E. ADAMS NEELY, JR.
E. L. HAYWOOD   ARTHUR G. PEELER
                W. GREGG SUTTON

Class of 1932
HENRY BELL BENOIT   JOHN B. PESCHAU
ADLAI H. ELIASON   LOUIS SHERFESEE
JAMES A. HUDSON   FRANK WILLARD SLUSSER
ERNEST W. KING   AMOS HILL TAYLOR
JOSEPH FALLS MORRIS   SAGE H. UPSHAW
WILLARD LEE PARRISH   WILLIAM A. WITHERS

Law
LeROY WELLS ARMSTRONG   EDWARD SCHEIDT
                A. K. SMITH

Medicine
PAUL GREGG WEIL

Pledges
LUCAS ABELS   PHILLIP PEACOCK
JOHN D. BRANCH   LEE RICHARDSON
JAMES H. KRIDER   LeROY JOHNSON
                A. C. SKINNER

BROOKER	BROWN	ERICKSON	GARLAND
GRIER	GILBERT	GRANT	G.L.JONES
H.F.JONES	LITTLE	NELSON	PARKER
QUINN	SIEDER	SLOOP	WOODWARD

ALPHA TAU OMEGA

Founded at Virginia Military Institute, 1865

Colors: Old Gold and Sky Blue   *Flower*: White Tea Rose

Publication: The Palm

Alpha Delta Chapter

Established 1879

Fratres in Facultate

THOMAS J. WILSON, JR., PH.D.   ATWELL C. McINTOSH, A.M.
EUGENE C. BRANSON, A.M.   GERALD R. McCARTHY, A.M.
HARRY F. COMER   THOMAS S. McCORKLE
WM. D. MacMILLAN, PH.D.   WILLIAM R. ABBOT, A.M.
HOWARD R. HUSE   KEENER C. FRASER, PH.D.
FLETCHER McLUIN GREEN

Fratre in Urbe

JOSEPH HYDE PRATT

Fratres in Universitate

Class of 1931

HERBERT A. NELSON   GEORGE J. QUINN
CHARLES P. ERICKSON   B. A. SIEDER
PAUL L. GILBERT   THOMAS GRIFFIN

Class of 1932

CHARLES K. WOODWARD   LELAND W. SALE
WILLIAM GORDON BOGER   BARRON K. GRIER
LOFTON P. BROOKER   H. FRED JONES
KENNETH MARLAND

Law

F. OGDEN PARKER   B. THORN LORD
T. CARLISLE SMITH, JR.   ALLSTON J. STUBBS

Medicine

RUFUS R. LITTLE

Pledges

GEORGE JONES   JOE GANT
JOHN SLOOP   CHESTER BROWN
PETER GARLAND

ALLEN   CARPENTER   CARR

DANIEL   GARRETT   HOWELL   HUGHES   LINDSAY

LITTLE   MANN   MILLENDER   MORRISON   OLIVER

PEACE   PERKINS   REDDING   TALMADGE   TAYLOR

WARD   WATKINS   WELLS

[238]

KAPPA ALPHA

Founded at Washington and Lee University, 1856

Colors: Crimson and Gold   *Flowers*: Red Rose and Magnolia

Publications: Kappa Alpha Journal, Special Messenger (Secret)

Upsilon Chapter of Kappa Alpha

Fratres in Facultate

HOWARD W. BAILEY, A.B.   J. G. DER. HAMILTON, PH.D.
EDGAR W. KNIGHT, PH.D.

Fratres in Universitate

Class of 1930

STEPHEN H. MILLENDER   DAVID J. WARD
EUGENE E. WELLS

Class of 1931

WILLIAM G. CARR, JR.   WILLIAM S. LINDSAY
HOWARD R. GARRETT   ARTHUR D. LITTLE, JR.
JOSEPH DER. HAMILTON, JR.   WILLIAM B. OLIVER

Class of 1932

FRANK A. COLE, JR.   ALONZO R. PERKINS, JR.
SAMUEL T. PEACE, JR.   THOMAS H. REDDING

Law

OSCAR B. CARPENTER   HUGH L. LOBDELL

Medicine

HARRY E. TALMADGE

Graduates

JOHN C. HERBERT   FRANK S. HOWELL
ROBERT M. WALLACE

Pledges

BURWELL A. ALLEN   EDWARD B. MANN
STEPHEN W. CARPENTER   JAMES S. MORRISON
JOHN W. DANIEL   WILLIAM W. TAYLOR
ALFRED T. HAMILTON   WILLIAM L. TROTTER
ROLFE E. HUGHES   THOMAS WATKINS

BARNES

BUNN

CLELAND

C.C.DALEY

W.A.DALEY

DANIELS

DeWOLFE

EWBANK

FONVIELLE

GRANTHAM

GRIFFIN

KNOWLES

MARSHALL

MARTINDALE

MEACHAM

MILLS

NEWLAND

J.G.PEACOCK

J.T.PEACOCK

TAYLOR

THOMAS

PHI DELTA THETA
Founded at Miami University, 1848

Colors: Argent and Azure   *Flower*: White Carnation

Publications: The Scroll and The Palladium

N. C. Beta Chapter of Phi Delta Theta
Established 1885

Fratres in Facultate

WILLIAM S. BERNARD, A.M.
C. T. McCORMICK, A.B., LL.B.
WILLIAM P. BRANDON, A.M.

PATRICK H. WINSTON, A.B.
WILLIAM F. PROUTY, PH.D.
THOMAS F. HICKERSON, PH.D.

Fratres in Universitate

Class of 1930

PHILLIP L. THOMAS   ERNEST W. EWBANK
GEORGE R. BENTON, JR.

Class of 1931

LEWIS E. SCOGGINS   WILLIAM R. MILLS
WALTER ALEX DALEY   THOMAS M. CLELAND
HORACE M. BARNES   DANIEL CHARLES DeWOLFE
WILLIAM P. FREEZE

Class of 1932

TAD L. MCLAUGHLIN   CARROLL H. KOONCE
EDWARD MOSELY FONVIELLE   JAMES P. BUNN, JR.
E. D. GILL   THOMAS EDMUNDS MARSHALL

Pledges

ELBERT C. DANIEL, JR.   RODNEY KNOWLES, JR.
NORMAN GRANTHAM   HOWARD MARTINDALE
JULIEN K. TAYLOR, JR.   HOWARD T. NEWLAND
KENNETH T. WHITE   JOHN PEACOCK
HASEL L. MEACHAM   THOMAS PEACOCK
JONATHAN W. JACKSON   WILLIAM H. GRIFFIN

ALLEN   CARR   COOPER   CRAWFORD

DAMERON   G.W. HAMER   E.R. HAMER   HEDGPETH   HENDERSON

HINES   LONDON   MARSHALL   MILLER   MURPHY

PALMORE   PARK   PERSON   RAMSAY   REDFERN

SIKES   C.C. SKINNER   J.G. SKINNER   UNDERHILL   WADSWORTH

SIGMA NU

Founded at Virginia Military Institute, 1868

Colors: Black, White and Gold   *Flower*: White Rose

Publication: The Delta of Sigma Nu

Psi Chapter of Sigma Nu
Established 1888

Fratres in Facultate

HARRY W. CHASE, PH.D.
WILLIAM D. MCNIDER, M.D.
S. M. BRECKENBRIDGE, PH.B.

CLARENCE A. HIBBARD, A.M.
EARLE E. PEACOCK, A.M.
A. HENDERSON, PH.D., LL.D.

C. C. PEACOCK, A.M.
J. B. WOOSLEY, A.M.
J. C. LYONS, PH.D.

Fratres in Universitate

Class of 1930

ARCH T. ALLEN, JR.
FREDERICK L. CARR, JR.
GEORGE W. HAMER
THADDEUS V. HEDGPETH

ROBERT L. MURPHY
JULIAN I. PALMORE
CHARLES M. REDFERN
WINGATE E. UNDERHILL

Class of 1931

EMERSON P. DAMERON
DONALD W. GRAHAM
EDWARD R. HAMER

WILLIS I. HENDERSON
EUGENE G. HINES, JR.
E. COOPER PERSON, JR.
JOHN G. WADSWORTH

CHARLES C. SIKES
KERR CRAIGE RAMSAY
CHARLES C. SKINNER, JR.

Class of 1932

A. BRANCH CARR
JOHN PHIL COOPER
WILLIAM C. CRAWFORD
WALTER M. CROUCH

LAWRENCE B. JOHNSON
HENRY M. LONDON, JR.
LAWRENCE L. MILLER
JOHN A. PARK, JR.

JAMES G. SKINNER
W. IVERSON SKINNER
CHARLES H. WHEDBEE
MARION B. THOMAS

Law

CHARLES PRICE   WILLIAM L. MARSHALL, JR.

Graduates

WALTER D. CREECH   JAMES B. MCMILLIAN

Pledges

FRANK BENNETT, JR.
JAMES HARRY BUNN
CHARLES STUART CARR
EDWIN BROWN DAVIS
EDWARD BENJAMIN FERGUSON

CHARLES SUTTLE FORBES
JOHN SADLER HAYES
JAMES THOMAS GRIFFITH
WALTER AUSTEN LANE
GEORGE ELLIOT LONDON

WILLIAM CRUMP MCCORKLE
JAMES MCKINNEY MOYE
ARNOLD HOLMES SNIDER
LOUIS CHERRY SKINNER
THOMAS HASELL WRIGHT

BENJAMIN CLIFTON PRINCE   LENOIR CHAMBERS WRIGHT

ABERNETHY   ADAMS   ADKINS   BULLUCK   BUNN   CARLISLE

CATE   CHANDLER   DOCKERY   GARRETT   HENRY   HINES

HOLCOMB   HOLE   HUNTER   JACOCKS   J.B.JARRATT   A.H.JARRATT

KARLE   LIPSCOMB   LYNCH   MILLS   PEACOCK   PETTY

ROYSTER   J.C.SHELTON   T.M.SHELTON   SHUFORD   SICKLES   STATON

STIKELEATHER   THOMPSON   WALL   WHITE   WILSON   WOOD

SIGMA CHI

Founded at Miami University, June 28, 1885

Colors: Blue and Gold   *Flower*: White Rose

Publication: The Magazine of Sigma Chi

Alpha Tau of Sigma Chi

Established 1889

Fratres in Facultate

HERMAN G. BAITY, M.S.
FREDERICK H. KOCH, A.M.
JAMES JERRY SLADE, M.S.
R. P. McCLAMROCK, PH.D.

WESLEY C. GEORGE, PH.D.
WILLIAM N. EVANS, JR., LL.B.
JOHN W. LASLEY, JR., PH.D.
JAMES F. ROYSTER, PH.D.

FREDERICK B. McCALL, LL.B.

Fratre in Urbe

WILLIAM D. SCOTT

Fratres in Universitate

Class of 1930

FENTON ANDREW ADKINS
WILLIAM LUMSTEN FEARING
THOMAS ALLISON HUNTER

LEONARD HOWLETT HOLE
LOY DURANT THOMPSON
ADOLPHUS MITCHELL

JOHN CRAIG SHELTON
WILLIAM LYTCH CARLISLE
AUGUSTUS HENRY JARRETT, JR.

Class of 1931

NICHOLA WEST DOCKERY
GEORGE FRANCIS JACOCKS

CHAUNCY LAKE ROYSTER
EDWIN RUSSEL LIPSCOMB

ARTHUR DeLOSS SICKLES
BONNER MILLS

Class of 1932

CLARENCE VERNON BARKLEY, JR.
JOHN GRAY BLOUNT ELLISON
STEVEN ANDREW LYNCH, JR.
WILLIAM TURRELIUS MYERS

WILLIAM CALVIN PETTY, JR.
WALTER THOMAS ROSE
THOMAS M. SHELTON, JR.
EDWIN CRAIG WALL

Medicine

WILLIAM MEBANE   AMOS NEILL JOHNSON

Law

JESSE SPENCER BELL   GLENN TERREBLE GARRATT
JOHN DAVID BULLUCK, JR.

Pledges

JOHN S. ADAMS
TORGLER F. ADKINS
JOHN M. ABERNETHY
TURNER B. BUNN
ARLINDO S. CATE
STUART M. CHANDLER

DAVID P. HENRY
WILMER M. HINES
HENRY WOOD, III
CHARLES E. HOLCOMB
J. BRUCE JARRATT
WILLIAM H. KARLE

JAMES W. PEACOCK
JACOB H. SHUFORD
A. HAROLD STATON
JAMES G. STIKELEATHER
WILLIAM L. WHITE
W. HOWARD WILSON

BAGBY   BRIDGERS   J.L.BROWN   R.A.BROWN   COZART

DAVIS   DUNN   EAGLES   FINCH   FORD   GEITNER

GRAY   HENDERSON   HOFFMAN   HOUSTON   KLEEMIERE   LANDIS

OLIVER   PELTON   PHILPOTT   ROSEMOND   SATTERFIELD   SHEMWELL

STAPLES   TOMS   WARE   WEBB   WHITE

KAPPA SIGMA
Founded at the University of Bologna, 1400
Established in America at the University of Virginia, 1867

Colors: Scarlet, White and Emerald Green   *Flower:* Lily of the Valley
Publications: Caduceus, and Star and Crescent (Secret)

Alpha Mu Chapter
Established 1893

Fratres in Facultate

JOHN GROVER BEARD, PH.D.
GUSTAVE M. BRAUNE, B.S., C.E.
ROBERT A. FETZER, B.S., M.A.
ELMER G. HOEFER, B.S., M.E.

STURGIS E. LEAVITT, PH.D.
MARCUS C. S. NOBLE, PH.D.
CHARLES THOMAS WOOLLEN
E. J. WOODHOUSE, A.B., LL.B.

Fratre in Urbe
GEORGE EDWARD SHEPARD

Fratres in Universitate

Class of 1930
FRANCIS ROGERS TOMS

Class of 1931

GEORGE LEWIS BAGBY
JOHN LEONARD BROWN, JR.
WILLIAM CLYDE DUNN
GEORGE PARROTT ROSEMOND

JOSEPH COLIN EAGLES
CHARLES ELLIS FORD
PETER LELAND HENDERSON

Class of 1932

WILLIAM ASHBY BRIDGERS
SYDNOR MOYE COZART
JOHN ELISHA DAVIS
HARRY CLINTON FINCH

ROBERT WALKER GEITNER
GEORGE PHIFER HOUSTON
JOEL JENKINS HUTCHINSON, JR.
JOHN AUGUSTUS KLEIMIERE

ROBERT SILLS OVERMAN
WILLIAM GORDON REID
WILLIAM ROBERT SATTERFIELD
GEORGE HUNTER WARE

Law
ROBERT MCDONALD GRAY, JR.

Medicine
ROBERT MITCHELL OLIVER   RICHARD WINBORNE, JR.

Pledges

RUFUS ALEXANDER BROWN
JAMES POLK GRAY
WILLIAM RHYNE HOFFMAN
PLATT WALKER LANDIS
ROY ARNOLD MCDADE

PAUL PHILLIP PELTON
BENJAMIN CABELL PHILPOTT
EVERARD BAXTER SHEMWELL
ERNEST W. STAPLES, JR.
EUGENE LEE WEBB, JR.

THOMAS SKINNER WHITE

| ASHCRAFT | BISANAR | CASSADA | CLARK | FRENCH |

| GORRELL | HINES | R.E.L.HOLT | W.K.HOLT | HOUSTON |

| HOWLEY | LOWRANCE | MARSHALL | McCOY | McNAIR |

| MOODY | PATTERSON | PHILLIPS | SAWYER | SHANER |

| SHUFORD | THOMPSON | WORNOM | WEEKS | WILLIAMS |

PI KAPPA ALPHA

Founded at University of Virginia, 1868

Colors: Garnet and Old Gold   *Flower*: Lily of the Valley

Publications: Shield and Diamond, Dagger and Key (Secret)

Tau Chapter of Pi Kappa Alpha
Established 1895

Fratres in Facultate

GUSTAVE A. HARRER, PH.D.   GEORGE McF. McKIE, A.M.
HOWARD M. JONES, PH.D.   JOHN E. CARROL, JR., A.M.
HENRY F. HUNT, M.D.

Fratres in Universitate

Class of 1930

FRANCIS MARION HOUSTON   EDWARD LEMUEL PATTERSON
JAMES LYTCH McNAIR, JR.

Class of 1931

JOHN BULLA ASHCRAFT   ALBERT THROSSELL HICKIN
ANDREW TYER SAYER   HARRY LINDEN SHANER, JR.
ROBERT EDWARD LEE HOLT, JR.   CHARLES STOWE MOODY

Class of 1932

GEORGE EDWARD FRENCH, JR.   ADRAIN SHUFORD, JR.
RICHARD WILSON MARSHALL   TOM WHITE WEEKS
ANTON ALEXANDER PHILLIPS   LAWSON HENRY LOWRANCE
HORACE HINES   WARD THOMPSON

Law

HOWARD LACKEY   HENRY ROANE
CLAY CARTER STUDDERT

Pledges

JOHN ANGIER BLUE   JOHN SHELTON GORRELL
EDGAR ALAN BISANAR   CLARENCE LATIMER McCOY, JR.
CLAUDE BAXTER CLARK, JR.   RICHARD SPENCER STUDDERT
WILLIAM K. HOLT, JR.   HARVAY CLINTON BRADY
JOHN WATKINS WILLIAMS, JR.   HARRY HALLECK CASSADA
RICHARD NEELY BARBER, JR.   FRANK MORTON HAWLEY
VACHEL THOMAS CHEARS, JR.   ALEX HUDGINS WORNOM

ADAMS   BANNER   BOBBITT   BOREN

BROWN   DANIEL   DAVIS   GHOLSON   GILBREATH

GILLESPIE   GRAVES   HOYLE   KOCHTITSKY   MARTIN

McINNIS   McLEOD   MOORE   NEWMAN   O'NEIL

PLEASANTS   RAND   SLATER   WILLIAMS   WIMBISH.

PI KAPPA PHI

Founded at the College of Charleston, 1904

Colors: Gold and White   *Flower*: Red Rose

Publications: Star and Lamp of Pi Kappa Phi, Fokromix (Esoteric)

Kappa Chapter of Pi Kappa Phi

Established 1914

Fratres in Facultate

DUDLEY DEW. CARROLL, A.M.   CORYDON P. SPRUILL, LITT.B.   WILLIAM OLSEN, M.A.
JEFFERSON C. BYNUM, M.S.   (OXON)   WILLIAM GRADY PRITCHARD

Fratres in Universitate

Class of 1930

CHARLES W. BANNER, JR.   FRANK CHURCH O'NEIL
WILLIAM EDGAR BOBBITT   JOHN ALBERT VANN, JR.
ERNEST CLEWELL McINNIS

Class of 1931

THURSTON RAY ADAMS   KERMIT WAYNE WELBORN   MARSHALL DUSKIN RAND
ARTHUR HUGH MARTIN   ALLEN COOK BOREN   BEVERLY COOPER MOORE
CLIFTON EDWARD PLEASANTS GEORGE F. NEWMAN, JR.   OLLEN D. McLEOD
JOHN GARY SLATER   PAUL CUNNINGHAM WIMBISH

Class of 1932

THERON REMFRY BROWN   CHARLES MARTIN FARMER
THOMAS PITTMAN DAVIS   JAMES BASTER DAWSON, JR.
JOHN McIVER GILLESPIE   JOHN ULPIN GILBREATH
ADRIAN NATHAN DANIEL, JR. OSCAR WILBUR KOCHTITSKY, JR.

Law

WALTER MOORE BRYSON   ALFRED WADDELL GHOLSON, JR.   JOHN FRAZIER GLENN, JR.
CALVIN GRAVES, JR.   WALTER HOYLE   HENRY THRUMAN POWELL

Medicine

WILLIAM O'KELLY FOWLER   JAMES BROWNLEE HALL, JR.   ROBERT WALLACE WILKINS

Graduates

ROBERT WALLER ACHURCH   AUBREY ALONZO PERKINS   JAMES WILLIAM WILLIAMS

Pledges

HARPER BARNES   WILLIAM N. DIXSON, JR.   FENNER TILDEN PHILLIPS
HENRY ARMISTEAD BOYD   BERNICE D. FARMER, JR.   SCHUYLER C. SCHENCK, IV
CHARLES HERIOT BRAWLEY   MOODY ZIMRIA GAITHER, JR.   GEORGE A. PHILLIPS, JR.
WAYLAND C. BUCHANAN   JAMES GORDON KURFEES   JAMES HAROLD SMITH
WILLIAM WOODARD WALKER   BUXTON BARKER WILLIAMS, JR.

BATTLEY   BROWN   CARLTON   CHAMBERLAIN

CORNWALL   DUFFY   GILLIES   HESTER   JOHNSON

KETCHIE   K.L.KJELLESVIG   P.P.KJELLESVIG   KOEHL   MARSHALL

MERRITT   RAYMER   REYNOLDS   ROTH   STARBUCK

G.H.STURM   M.S.STURM   THOMAS   WATKINS

DELTA SIGMA PHI

Founded at the College of the City of New York, 1899

Colors: White, Nile Green and White   *Flower*: White Carnation

Publications: The Carnation (Exoteric), The Sphinx (Esoteric)

Alpha Delta Chapter

Established 1920

Fratres in Facultate

WALTER REESE BERRYHILL   MAURICE TAYLOR VAN HECKE

Fratre in Urbe

DOUGLAS McINTOSH FAMBROUGH

Fratres in Universitate

Class of 1930

WILLIAM HOWARD BROWN   MILTON STANLEY STURM
ROBERT C. MERRITT, JR.   JAMES KEEFE WARD

Class of 1931

CHARLES CHAPMAN DUFFY   ALAN ASHWORTH MARSHALL
COWN CARSON FOARD   BARRON LLOYD RITCHIE
JOSEPH FAIRFIELD HESTER   WILLIAM AGURS STARBUCK
PEDRO PABLO KJELLESVIG   WILLIAM ARCHIE SUGG
GEORGE MARTIN KOEHL   FRED AMICK THOMAS
JOSEPH PAXTON WATKINS, JR.

Class of 1932

WILLIAM RICHARD BATTLEY   KOLBEIN LUDWIG KJELLESVIG
RICHARD M. CHAMBERLAIN   DEWEY LITTLE RAYMER
CHARLES CASTNER CORNWALL   LOWELL THOMAS WELLS
HANSEL DALTON KETCHIE   GORDON HOUSTON STURM

Law

RODOPH DUFFY   CLAUDE EVERETT REITZEL

Graduate

CARL VERNON FARRISS

Pledges

CHARLES WALTON CARLTON   JOHN W. REYNOLDS, JR.
HARRY GLENN FRAZIER   RODERICK McLEOD GILLIES
CLARENCE E. JOHNSON   WILLIAM LOWE ROTH
THOMAS BROWN WATKINS

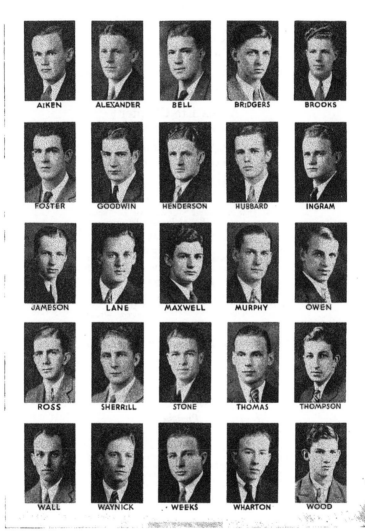

AIKEN   ALEXANDER   BELL   BRIDGERS   BROOKS

FOSTER   GOODWIN   HENDERSON   HUBBARD   INGRAM

JAMESON   LANE   MAXWELL   MURPHY   OWEN

ROSS   SHERRILL   STONE   THOMAS   THOMPSON

WALL   WAYNICK   · WEEKS   WHARTON   WOOD

THETA CHI
Founded at Norwich University, 1856

Colors: Military Red and White　　　　　　　*Flower:* Red Carnation

Publication: The Rattle

Alpha Eta Chapter
Established 1920

Fratres in Facultate
SAMUEL HUNTINGTON HOBBS

Fratres in Universitate

Class of 1930
J JOHNSTON ALEXANDER　　　WILLIAM E. ANGLIN
J. ROBERT INGRAM, JR.

Class of 1931
JOSEPH K. RAY　　　　　　KENNETH A. BELL
JAMES CLIVIE GOODWIN　　NEILL A. THOMPSON
E. FRANK THOMAS　　　　　J. VASSIE WILSON, JR.

Class of 1932
D. RUSSELL FOSTER　　　　RAY HENDERSON
HARLAN JAMESON　　　　　JOSEPH D. ROSS, JR.
JACK L. SHERRILL　　　　　O. HAYWOOD WEEKS

Law
LAWRENCE J. GILES, JR.　　R. PARKER WAYNICK, JR.

Medicine
WILLIAM S. WALL

Graduate
VERNON L. WHARTON

Pledges
CHARLES AIKEN　　　　　　EMORY MARVEL
RONALD BROOKS　　　　　　W. H. MAXWELL
CHARLES BOYD　　　　　　　G. S. MURPHEY
KELLY BRIDGERS　　　　　　O. CLYDE OWEN, JR.
THOMAS A. GLASCOCK　　　EDWARD RATCLIFFE
ROBERT HUBBARD　　　　　MARION F. STONE
STATON MCIVER　　　　　　WILLIAM H. VANEVERY
B. B. LANE　　　　　　　　DOUGLAS WOOD
WAVERLY WHITE

| ARMFIELD | DOUGHTIE | FEREBEE | FOUNTAIN | GAULT |

| HEINITSH | HILLER | JACKSON | KAPP | KLUTZ |

| MILLER | MOCK | PICKETT | POND | C.D. ROLLINS |

| V. B. ROLLINS | SCALES | SHAFFNER | SMALL | SMITH |

| SNYDER | STULTZ | WADDILL | WEIS | WHEARY |

DELTA TAU DELTA
Founded at Bethany College, 1859

Colors: Purple, White and Gold   *Flower*: Pansy

Publication: The Rainbow

Gamma Omega Chapter
Established 1921

Fratres in Facultate

HAROLD D. MEYER   CHARLES DALE BEERS

Fratres in Universitate

Class of 1930

PHILIP JACKSON   EDMOND LAW WADDILL
THOMAS M. SNYDER

Class of 1931

JERRY WHITSETT DOUGHTIE   JOSEPH P. FOX
JAMES L. FEREBEE   WALLACE BRYAN SCALES
EMIL NATHANIEL SHAFFNER   KERMIT WHEARY
RICHARD B. ARMFIELD

Class of 1932

C. HEGE KAPP   CHARLES D. ROLLINS
C. GLENN MOCK   HENRY J. STULTZ, JR.
JOHN MARION MILLER   FRED E. ATIYEH

Law

JAMES H. CHADBOURN   WILLIAM D. POPE SHARPE, JR.

Medicine

GEORGE W. HEINITSH   VANCE B. ROLLINS

Pledges

J. EMERSON FOUNTAIN   LAURENCE PICKETT
CHARLES GAULT   HARRY R. SMALL
RICHARD HILLER   J. HAROLD SMITH
CHARLES H. KLUTTZ   CAMERON WEEKS
R. CAFFREY POND   GILBERT O. WEIS

ALEXANDER   AYCOCK   CAIN   CALDWELL

EIGHME   GUNTER   HALL   HAMMOND   · HARPER

JOHNSON   JOHNSTON   ·KARRIKER   LINN   MAGNER

MERRELL   MIXSON   PARKER   PORTER   ·REAVES

REDDING   SAPP   TEMPLE   YANCEY

SIGMA PHI EPSILON

Founded at the University of Richmond, 1901

Colors: Purple and Red   *Flowers*: American Beauties and Violets

Publication: Sigma Phi Epsilon Journal

North Carolina Delta Chapter
Established 1921

Fratres in Universitate

Class of 1930

John H. Dougherty
Sanford C. Harper, Jr.
L. Erastus Reves, Jr.
Ashley F. Seawell, Jr.

Class of 1931

June U. Gunter
Lawrence T. Hammond
Malcolm B. Seawell
Thurman R. D. Karriker
Herman S. Merrell

Class of 1932

Ben T. Aycock
Maurice Eighme
Pat H. Johnson
B. B. Forrest
R. Henry Temple
Sam M. Yancey

Law

Marion R. Alexander
Hall Blackstock
James Birney Linn
James Edward Magner
B. Moore Parker
Clarence Odell Sapp

Pledges

Fred Cain
Allen Caldwell
Paul Cooper
James Crews
Simmons Mixon
Charles Cheek
William Hall
Earl Higdon
Jesse Johnston
Thomas Johnston
John Latham
Marvin Porter
Thomas Redding
Donald Seawell

BREEN   BROWN   COATES   J.COHEN

R.COHEN   EISNER ..   FELSHIN   GLABERSON   LEVY

MARPET.   ·NEIMAN   PERES   SHER   HIRSCH ..

SOSNIK   SPITZER   SULKIN   VOLKMAN   WARSHAUER

TAU EPSILON PHI
Founded at Columbia University, 1909

Colors: Lavender and White   *Flowers*: Lily of the Valley and Violets

Publication: The Plume

Omega Chapter of Tau Epsilon Phi
Established 1924

Fratres in Universitate

Class of 1930

JUDAH SHOHAN

Class of 1931

ARTHUR R. MARPET   DAVID NEIMAN
PHILIP SHER

Class of 1932

SAMUEL J. BREEN   RAYMOND COHEN
NESTOR Y. SOSNIK

Law

SEON FELSHIN   JEROME J. COHEN

Pledges

EDWARD BRENNER   THEODORE D. LEVY
GEORGE BROWN   I. E. PERES
NORMAN N. COATES   LAWRENCE E. SPITZER
JOSEPH EISNER   GEORGE SULKIN
SAMUEL GLABERSON   SAMUEL E. WARSHAUER
SIDNEY L. HIRSCH   NATHAN VOLKMAN

ADAMS   BAKER   R.B.CHEEK   J.M.CHEEK

CRANE   CULPEPPER   DANIELS   DOUGHTON   HENRY

HUNTER   JOHNSTON   JONES   LUFTY   MIDGETT

SOUTHERLAND   VAUGHAN   WALCK   WILSON   WYRICK

THETA KAPPA NU
Founded at Drury College, 1924

Colors: Argent, Crimson and Gold   *Flower*: White Rose

Publication: Theta News

N. C. Gamma Chapter

Fratre in Facultate
L. M. BROOKS, PH.D.

Fratres in Universitate

Class of 1930
SHELTON BRINSON HUNTER   FRED ODELL JOHNSTON
FRANK ALLEN JONES   NAPOLEON BONAPARTE LUFTY
                JAMES R. MAUS

Class of 1931
FRANCIS MARVIN ADAMS   FRED JENNINGS SOUTHERLAND
MERRIT CLARENCE BAKER   JOHN SOUTHGATE VAUGHAN
CHARLES HOWARD HENRY   CHARLES LLOYD WYRICK
                HILLIARD BAXLEY WILSON

Class of 1932
JOHN MORGAN CHEEK   RALPH BRYANT CHEEK
JAMES EMMET DOUGHTON   LORIMER W. MIDGETT

Pledges
THOMAS PENN CRANE   THOMAS PHILLIPS ISBELL
EDWIN M. CULPEPPER   CLAUDE WILLIAM WALCK
CHARLES GRAHAM DANIELS   STEVEN WALL

BORING   CRISCO   CRUTCHFIELD   DAVIS

C.H. FISHER   R.B. FISHER   GILBERT   HINKLE   HOLLAND

ISENHOUR   MASHBURN   RULFS   SHELTON   SOWERS

TAYLOR   WALL   WHITEHEART   WINECOFF

ALPHA LAMBDA TAU

Founded at Oglethorpe University, 1916

Colors: Black and Gold   *Flower*: American Beauty Rose

Publication: The Rose Leaf

Epsilon Chapter

Established 1925

Fratre in Facultate

E. K. PHYLER, PH.D.

Fratres in Universitate

Class of 1930

E. ROBERT DAVIS   THEODORE R. KEITH
HARRY M. GILBERT   ALEX MENDENHALL

Class of 1931

HOWARD F. CHRISCO   ROSCOE B. FISHER
COLBERT F. CRUTCHFIELD   ARMONDO M. PEREZ
JOSEPH C. FAULKNER   WALLACE SHELTON
CARL H. FISHER   PHILLIP K. SOWERS

Class of 1932

JOHN HENRY ISENHOUR   WILL R. TAYLOR, JR.

Pledges

HAMPTON W. BORING   THOMAS M. MASHBURN
CHARLES F. CREWS   DONALD J. RULFS
WARD L. HINKLE   WILLIAM S. WALL
MAX W. HOLLAND   G. LEE WHITEHEART
        GEORGE M. WINECOFF

BOWMAN   CONNOLLY   FLEMING

HEWITT   HOUSEHOLDER   H.R. MILLER   J.E. MILLER

PREVOST   ROBERTS   SPELL

STOWE   STUTZ   WALKER

LAMBDA CHI ALPHA

Founded at Boston College, 1909

Colors: Purple, Green and Gold   *Flower*: Violet

Publications: Purple, Green and Gold, Cross and Crescent

Gamma Nu Zeta

Established 1922

Fratres in Facultate

R. C. BULLOCK ·   A. K. KING
KARL H. FUSSLER   R. R. POTTER

Fratres in Universitate

Class of 1930

CAMERON CARDWELL MEADOR   M. GREER STUTZ
JACK RAYMOND MURPHY   THOMAS ROGER WALKER

Class of 1931

FRANK J. HOUSEHOLDER, JR.   JOHN AARON PREVOST
EDWIN G. LONG, JR.   WHITNER HARRIS PREVOST
            JOHN DANIEL WALTERS

Class of 1932

HOWARD GRAYDON BOWMAN   HUBERT RUSSELL MILLER
JOHN CALHOUN CONNOLLY   JOHN EDWARD MILLER
            JAMES B. SPELL

Pledges

RALPH FLEMING   CHARLES STOWE
MACON HEWITT   WADE STANLEY
PHILIP PADGETT   RUDOLPH ROBERTS

BRIGGS　　BRUNJES　　CARPENTER　　DIKE

J.B.FARRIS　　R.S.FARRIS　　FORD　　GEIGER　　GIBBONS

GRAY　　GUTHRIE　　HAMER　　KIDD　　LOFTIN

LOVELAND　　MOUNT　　REA　　SHOEMAKER　　C.G.TODD

C.L.TODD　　TUNSTALL　　VAN ECHOP　　WALFORD　　zurBURG

SIGMA PHI SIGMA

Founded at University of Pennsylvania, 1908

Colors: White and Gold   *Flowers*: Daffodils and Lily of the Valley

Publication: The Monad

Xi Chapter of Sigma Phi Sigma

Established 1926

Fratres in Facultate

OTTO STUHLMAN, JR., PH.D.   WILL DOCKERY MERRITT, M.S.

Fratre in Urbe

BILL CARBINE, JR.

Fratres in Universitate

Class of 1930

JOHN HENRY BRUNJES   WILLIAM GORDON DIKE
RAY SIMPSON FARRIS   JOHN FRED FORD
SAM STEVENSON MCNEELY, JR.   RICHARD M. WALFORD, JR.
HENRY HERMANN ZURBURG

Class of 1931

JOSEPH ANDREW CARPENTER   ALFRED ALEXANDER MOUNT
GEORGE LUSCIUS SHERAM, JR.   EVAN JAMES VAUGHN

Class of 1932

VERNON LEWIS BRIGGS   JACK BRODIE FARRIS
CARL FRANCOIS GRIGGS   PAUL ALEXANDER GUTHRIE
EDWARD BENEDICT KIDD, JR.   LEWIS JOSEPH LOVELAND
CALVIN GRIER TODD   CALVIN LUTHER TODD
GEORGE LOUIS VANECHOP, JR.

Law

GREGORY ANDREW SMITH

Pledges

JOHN F. GEIGER   HENRY E. GIBBONS, JR.
DANIEL E. GRAY, JR.   JEROME HAMER
JOSEPH HINDS   CHARLES I. LOFTIN
THOMAS E. REA   J. REID SHOEMAKER
KENNETH R. TUNSTALL

ANDREWS   CLICK   COCHRANE   DENNING

DILLEHAY   EVANS   GUPTON   HANSCOMBE   JACKSON

JENKINS   JONES   MANN   McGLAMERY   MERRITT

MITCHELLE   PETREE   PHOENIX   PROCTER   SARTWELL

SCURLOCK   TEACHY   THOMAS   WHITTINGTON   WOOD

PHI SIGMA KAPPA

Founded at Massachusetts Agricultural College, Amherst, 1873

Color: Magenta   *Flower*: Red Carnation

Publication: The Signet

Upsilon Deuteron Chapter
Established 1926

Fratres in Facultate

R. B. Lawson   T. L. Kesler
F. C. Vilbrandt   C. J. McHale

Fratre in Urbe
John L. Holshouser

Fratres in Universitate

Class of 1930

J. P. Scurlock   W. T. Jackson, Jr.
E. H. Denning   C. H. White, Jr.
A. S. Mann, Jr.

Class of 1931

F. C. Thomas   W. H. McGlamery, Jr.
E. M. Fowler   Robert Hanscombe
Donald Wood   H. W. Jones
R. T. Proctor

Class of 1932

R. T. Jenkins   R. T. Sartwell
G. C. Cochrane   W. T. Fitzgerald
H. J. Dillehay   J. C. Teachey
L. O. Gupton   C. M. Andrew
R. J. Whittington, Jr.   C. B. Pheonix
D. M. McGlamery   M. M. Fitch

Law
Edmund L. Curlee

Medicine
Glenn S. Edgerton

Pledges

W. S. Petree   T. C. Evans, Jr.
C. M. Rives, Jr.   W. W. Peetz
W. E. Mitchelle   H. F. Click
J. F. Merritt   G. R. Vick

ABRAMS

AVNER

CONE

G. DANNENBAUM

R. DANNENBAUM

GALLAND

GUMP

KLEIN

MINTZ

PACHMAN

PERLSTINE

SPIGEL

STERNBERGER

WEIL

ZETA BETA TAU

Founded at the College of the City of New York, 1898

Colors: Gold, Blue and White

Alpha Pi Chapter
Established 1927

Fratres in Universitate

Class of 1930

DAVID L. AVNER   HARRY J. GALLAND

Class of 1931

SOLOMON B. STERNBERGER   DANIEL J. PACHMAN

Class of 1932

FLOYD J. PEARLSTINE   LIONEL B. WEIL, JR.
HARRY GUMP   GEORGE DANNENBAUM
NORMAN B. KLEIN   ROBERT DANNENBAUM

Pledges

HAROLD CONE   FRANK J. MANHEIM
JULIAN SPIGEL   SEYMOUR ABRAMS
            SEYMOUR MINTZ

AUSTIN BRISSON BROOKS N.E.BRYAN

N.L.BRYAN BUNCH COLEY CONRAD DAVIS FARRELL

FLYNT FRAZER GALLOWAY GREENE GRIFFIN JENSEN

LEA MARSH McCAMPBELL PARK PARKER PRICE

PURSER ROBINSON SCARBOROUGH SHEFFIELD SKEEN STAHR

STIMSON TUCKER WHICHARD WHISNANT WHITE YOUNG

SIGMA ZETA

Founded at the University of Michigan, 1924

Colors: Black and Gold   *Flower*: Pansy

Publication: The Torch of Sigma Zeta

Gamma Chapter
Established 1928

Fratre in Facultate
RUPERT BAYLISS VANCE, PH.D.

Fratres in Universitate

Class of 1930

RALPH CORDELLE GREENE
FRANK PHILIPS STIMSON
EUGENE LEARY
WILLIS GUILFORD WHICHARD
JOSEPH HERMAN BRISSON
WILLIAM JULIAN STONE
WALTER F. OWEN

Class of 1931

FRED BRENNING BUNCH, JR.
NORMAN LUTHER BRYAN, JR.
LEO BROWN SKEEN
JAMES LAWERENCE COLEY
JAMES HAROLD SHEFFIELD
HOWARD PRESTIN WHISNANT
GUS OBIE DAVIS
RANKIN JONES WHITE
MEBAN THOMAS LEA
MILTON PERCIVAL PARK

Class of 1932

CASPER MARION AUSTIN
ALDEN JOSEPH STAHR
STEPHEN PARKER MARSH
AVERETTE JACK MITCHELL
OSGOOD JEFFERSON YOUNG
CARL MILTON TUCKER. JR.
NORWOOD EASON BRYAN
EDWARD VICTOR CONRAD
FRANK WILSON FARRELL

Law

AGUSTUS McA. COVINGTON   HENRY BRYCE PARKER

Medicine

HENKLE M. PRICE

Pledges

BENJAMIN BARBER FRAZER
ENTIS TILDEN ROBINSON
CLARENCE ARTHUR JENSEN
JOSEY KAY GALLOWAY
ROMULUS HOKE FLYNT
JOSEPH ELMO HUFFMAN
THOMAS HENRY BROOKS
JOHN SPARKS GRIFFIN
JOHN CALDWELL McCAMPBELL
JOHN CLAYTON PURSER
CANFIELD SMITH DICKIE
BENJAMIN F. PARKER
VERNON HARRY SCARBOROUGH

ABELSON BESSEN

BRICK G.M.COHEN M.COHEN FLEISHMAN

GROSSMAN KRAMER KRASNY LEWIS

LIBERSTEIN LUBETKIN MARGULIES SILVERSTEIN

[2 7 6]

PHI ALPHA
Founded at George Washington University, 1914

Colors: Maroon and Blue   *Flower*: Rose

Publications: Phi Alpha Quarterly and Phi Alpha Bulletin (Esoteric)

Omega Chapter
Established 1928

Fratres in Universitate

Class of 1930

SIDNEY BRICK   HARRY GROSSMAN
GABRIEL M. COHEN   LEONARD D. LEWIS

Class of 1931

MILTON COHEN   HARRY KRAMER
            SAM SILVERSTEIN

Class of 1932

STANLEY B. ABELSON   ROBERT L. KUSHNER

Pledges

JACK BESSEN   HENRY LUBETKIN
MILTON FLEISHMAN   JACK MARGOLIS
SAMUEL GLASS   IRVING MARGULIES
MORRIS KRASNY   BENJAMIN MINSKER
WILLIAM LIBERSTEIN   ELIAS SELIGSON

BROWN   W.C.BURNETT   R.T.BURNETT   DRY

GROOME   GROSS   HENSLEY   LANE   LEAR

McCALL   MEHAFFEY   MOORE   NEWSOM   OVERMAN

PLUMMER   SMITH   SOUTHERLAND   STONE   WELLS

THETA PHI

Founded 1926

Colors: Orange and Blue   *Flower*: Sweet Pea

Fratres in Facultate

John E. Lear, E.E.   Ralph M. Trimble, C.E., M.S.

Fratres in Universitate

Class of 1930

William Clingan Burnett   William Herbert McCall
William Henry Dry   George Pryor Stone, Jr.
Charles Merritt Lear   John Robert Wells

Class of 1931

Ernest T. Gross, Jr.   Jesse Strickland Newsom
Charles A. Hensley, Jr.   Charles Beatty Overman
William Hooks Lane   Robert Cronly Plummer
Fred Joyner Moore   Pelham Powell Renfrow
                Robert Festus Welch

Class of 1932

Austin Newland Allen   Ivey Addison Groome
Callis Harvey Atkins   John P. Mehaffey
John Frederick Barrett   Hermit E. Smith
Albert Curtis Brown   William Odell Southerland
Robert Trafford Burnett   Ernest M. Whittington, Jr.

BRAINARD   CONNALLY   COVINGTON   CROOM

CURTIS   DUNGAN   HENRY   HODGES   HOLDER

HORNEY   McNAIRY   McPHERSON   MEBANE   POOLE

SHORE   SMITH   WEILAND   WILEY

SIGMA DELTA

Founded 1924

Colors: Brown and White   *Flower*: Cape Jessamine

Fratres in Facultate

JAMES O. BAILEY   HENRY N. DEWICK
WILLIAM T. COUCH   MURPHY D. RANSON

Fratres in Universitate

Class of 1930

HARRY J. BRAINARD   GARLAND MCPHERSON
GLEN P. HOLDER   JAMES G. POOLE
WILLIAM J. HORNEY   LAWRENCE P. STACK
JOHN MEBANE   SAMUEL WILEY
SAMUEL G. WINSTEAD

Class of 1931

MATTHEW GEORGE HENRY   JOHN CROOM
JAY CURTIS   SHERMAN SHORE

Class of 1932

SAMUEL H. AUSTIN   J. ELWIN DUNGAN
F. OSCAR CARVER   JAMES D. MCNAIRY, JR.
W. EUGENE CONNALY   JAMES WICKLIFFE SMITH
SAMUEL BYRD WINSTEAD

Law

DAVE THOMAS

Graduate

HAYWOOD PARKER, JR.

Pledges

LOUIS V. BROOKS   MORGAN P. MOORER
S. H. CRUMPLER   GEORGE W. THOMAS, JR.
W. V. COVINGTON   JAMES L. THOMAS
ALONZO M. LANSFORD   WILLIAM H. SPRADLIN, JR.
ROLAND LONG   HENRY WEILAND
ROBERT HODGES

BARBER   C.W. BLACKWOOD   J.C. BLACKWOOD   GOODE

GOODWIN   HARRELL   HEWITT   LAWRENCE

LOHR   LONG   McLAUGHLIN   PACE

SALES   SMITH   SPARKS   WHITLEY

SIGMA EPSILON

Founded at the University of North Carolina, 1924

Colors: Purple, Cerise and Gray   Flower: White Rose

Publication: Sigma Epsilon Scroll

Fratres in Facultate

J. WILLIS POSEY, A.M.
J. LEROY SMITH, A.M.

Fratres in Urbe

H. EDWARD THOMPSON, II   J. NELSON CALLAHAN
RICHARD A. FREEMAN

Fratres in Universitate

Class of 1930

CARL W. BLACKWOOD   G. HAROLD McCORMICK
GEORGE B. GOODE   DERMOT LOHR
LINWOOD P. HARRELL   CALVIN S. McLAUGHLIN
WILLIAM H. POTTER

Class of 1931

WILLIAM N. LAWRENCE   JACK W. SMITH
PAUL R. SPARKS   DOWD P. WHITLEY
J. CURTIS BLACKWOOD   CLEON W. GOODWIN
JOHN C. SALES

Class of 1932

B. GEORGE BARBER, JR.
WILLIAM E. UZZELL

Medicine

SAMUEL E. PACE

Pledges

WYNDHAM W. HEWITT   JOSEPH J LONG, JR.
FREDERICK C. KRAUSS   JERRY NEWTON

BARKLEY EDWARDS FUSSELL

LANG LOWRY. MATHEWS

RANKIN SWAIN WILLIAMS

PHI KAPPA DELTA

Founded 1926

Colors: White and Light Blue

Fratres in Universitate

Class of 1930

J. A. Lang   F. C. Rankin
R. F. Lowry   Minor Barkley
J. C. Williams

Class of 1931

C. O. Matthews   W. K. James
L. H. Fussell   E. L. Swain
D. C. Edwards   H. F. Turner
J. P. Sherrill

Class of 1932

N. E. Wiggins

Law

O. M. Smith

Pledges

F. D. Clawson   Deems Clifton
J. C. Cox   James Van Hoy

BUCK   CARTER

CURRIE   CURRY   DANIEL   FOOSHE'

GRADY   KITCHIN   MORRISETTE   MURPHY

NORCROSS   SHERARD   THACKER   WALL

CHI OMEGA

Founded at the University of Arkansas, 1895

Colors: Cardinal and Straw   *Flower*: White Carnation

Publication: Eleusis

Epsilon Beta Chapter

Established 1923

Sorores in Urbe

Mrs. Donald Coney	Mrs. J. C. Lyons
Mrs. R. D. W. Connor	Mrs. E. L. Mackie
Mrs. William T. Couch	Mrs. H. D. Meyer
Miss Nellie Graves	Mrs. W. W. Pierson, Jr.
Mrs. Guy Johnson	Miss Margaret Pritchard
Miss Estelle Lawson	Mrs. Wallace Smith

Sorores in Universitate

Class of 1930

Mary Price
Sidney Curry
Dorothy Fooshe

Class of 1931

Ruby Buck	Harriet Daniel
Mary Burroughs	Mary Norcross
Polly Carter	Edna Morrisette
Ida Currie	Kate Parks Kitchin

Graduates

Elizabeth Howland
Elizabeth Murphy
Katherine Sherard

Pledges

Elsie Grady
Louise Thacker
Louise Wall

BARBER   CARPENTER   COKER   CURRIE

DUNCAN   EDGERTON   FALKENER   FEASTER   FORESTER

GRAHAM   HARDING   HILL   MANGUM   McALISTER

McANALLY   McKAY   McKINNE   MELICK   MILMO

REED   TURNER   WAY   WITHERS

PI BETA PHI
Founded at Monmouth College, 1867

Colors: Wine and Silver Blue   *Flower*: Wine Carnation

Publication: The Arrow

North Carolina Alpha Chapter
Established 1923

Sorores in Urbe

KATHERINE BATTS	MRS. HARRY RUSSELL
ELIZABETH BRANSON	MRS. A. S. LAWRENCE
KATHERINE MARTIN	MRS. HUGO GIDDIS
GRACE DUNCAN	MRS. FRED MCCALL
ROSALIE THRALL	MRS. DOUGALD MACMILLAN
SUSAN ROSS	MRS. W. E. CALDWELL
MRS. HILL SHINE	MRS. EDWARD BROWN
MRS. H. F. COMER	

Sorores in Universitate

Class of 1930

ELIZABETH BARBER	SARA FALKENER
MARY LEWISE CARPENTER	MAURINE FORESTER
ELEANOR COKER	PHOEBE R. HARDING
ANNE KELSO CURRIE	HELEN MCKAY
CELESTE EDGERTON	ANNE C. MELICK
VIRGINIA M. MILMO	

Pledges

MARGARET BULLITT	ADELAIDE MCANALLY
KATE C. GRAHAM	ELZADA FEASTER
ADELAIDE REED	LILIE W. JACKSON
VIRGINIA TURNER	CLYDE DUNCAN
EDITH MANGUM	OLIVIA MCKINNE
MARY LAURENS WITHERS	EVELYN WAY
JOSEPHINE HILL	JEAN MACALLISTER

COWPER   FOWLER

HALL   HEINITH   LITTLE   OLIVER·

QUICKEL   ROLLINS   ROSE   SMITH

TURNER   WALL   WARD   WAY

PHI CHI

Founded at Louisville Medical School, 1893

Colors: Green and White   *Flower*: Lily of the Valley

Publication: Phi Chi Quarterly

Sigma Theta of Phi Chi

Established 1905

Fratres in Facultate

JAMES B. BULLET, M.D.   WILLIAM DEB. MACNIDER
WESLEY C. GEORGE, PH.D.   M.D.
W. REESE BERYHILL, M.D.

Fratre in Urbe

CALVERT T. TOY, M.D.

Fratres in Universitate

Second Year Medical Class

ROSCOE B. GRAY COWPER   VANCE BENTON ROLLINS
GLENN SAUNDERS EGERTON   AUGUSTUS STEELE ROSE
GEORGE W. HEINITSH   CLYDE TIMOTHY SMITH
RUFUS REID LITTLE   NEEDHAM EDGAR WARD
DUNCAN ROLAND MCEACHERN   JOHN CEPHAS QUICKEL

First Year Medical Class

JAMES BROWNLEE HALL, JR.   SAMUEL EASON WAY
WILLIAM O'KELLY FOWLER   WILLIAM STANLEY WALL
ROBERT MITCHELL OLIVER   JAMES ANNERTON TURNER, JR.
JAMES ALLEN WHITAKER   ROBERT WALLACE WILKINS

CALDWELL   FOX   FRITZ

GAY   HARRILL   KITCHEN

LUPTON   MOORE   PRICE

TOMLINSON   UPCHURCH   WILSON

THETA KAPPA PSI

Founded at the Medical College of Virginia, 1879

Colors: Nile Green and Old Gold   *Flower*: Red Rose

Publication: The Messenger

Upsilon Chapter
Established 1915

Fratres in Universitate

Class of 1930

C. C. Lupton   T. H. Tomlinson, Jr.
Frank Wilson, Jr.   T. G. Upchurch
L. M. Caldwell

Class of 1931

A. E. Barnhardt   H. W. Fox
J. W. Kitchen   W. A. Fritz
W. H. Flythe   H. M. Price
E. V. Moore   C. H. Gay
H. C. Harrell

ALEXANDER

ALLEN

ANDREW

BROWN

CLAPP

DAWSON

GARRISON

HUDSON

JOHNSON

KNOEFEL

McKEE

NORTHROP

PACE

RAMSAUR

SCARBOROUGH

STONE

STRICKLAND

TALMADGE

WANDECK

WESTMORELAND

WOODARD

ALPHA KAPPA KAPPA

Founded at Dartmouth College, 1889

Colors: Dartmouth Green and White   *Publication*: Centaur

Beta Iota Chapter

Established 1923

Fratres in Facultate

Dr. I. H. Manning
Dr. G. W. Carrington
Dr. Eric A. Abernethy

Fratres in Universitate

Second Year Medical Class

G. C. Allen
L. A. Andrew
L. G. Brown
H. L. Clapp
J. N. Dawson
G. L. Donnelly

C. F. Hudson
J. R. Johnson
S. E. Pace
L. J. Ring
A. T. Strickland
J. B. Westmoreland

First Year Medical Class

I. M. Alexander
D. M. Cogdell
R. B. Garrison
W. B. Green
A. E. Knoefel, Jr.

L. M. McKee
T. N. Northrop
J. T. Ramsaur
A. M. Scarborough
W. R. Wandeck

B. L. Woodard

Pledge

R. E. Stone

BOLTON

BAREFOOT

COBLE

REAVES

LEWIS

UMSTEAD

KAPPA PSI

Founded at the Medical College of Virginia, 1879

Colors: Scarlet and Gray   *Flower:* Red Carnation

Publications: The Mask (Exoteric), The Agoa (Esoteric)

Beta Xi Chapter
Established 1915

Fratres in Facultate

JOHN G. BEARD   EDWARD V. HOWELL
RALPH W. BOST   MARION L. JACOBS
          EDWARD V. KYSER

Fratres in Universitate

Class of 1930

ROBERT B. BALTON   OSCAR LOGAN UMSTEAD
RANCE EDWARD CLARK   LEO C. KELLY
MATT RANSON LEWIS   ROBERT GLENN KALE
JOE L. PINNIX   L. E. REAVES, JR.

Class of 1931

LEXIE G. BAREFOOT   AARON THOMAS GRIFFIN
JAMES CLIFFORD COBLE   BENJAMIN H. KENT
          PHILIP L. THOMAS

Pledges

MARTIN L. CLIVE   FRANK BENTON HAM
CLAYTON S. CURRY   A. D. EDENS
W. S. CROUCH   FREDERICK ROY, JR.
ARTHUR COCHRANE, JR.   L. R. McLELLAN

BOLEN　　BRASWELL　　BUNCH

CLODFELTER　　CRAIG　　CREECH　　DELLINGER

HICKS　　LIBBUS　　MOSS　　SISK

PHI DELTA CHI

Founded at the University of Michigan, 1883

Colors: Old Gold and Dregs of Wine   *Flower*: Red Carnation

Publication: The Communicator

Alpha Gamma Chapter
Established 1923

Fratres in Facultate

Honorary

H. Smith Richardson
Haywood M. Taylor

Fratres in Universitate

Class of 1930

H. E. Bolen	E. E. Merrill
T. A. Libbus	R. C. Sisk

Class of 1931

C. L. Clodfelter	T. G. Braswell
R. P. Craig	T. W. Gordon
H. M. Dellinger	A. L. Harris

Class of 1932

L. E. Bunch	G. A. Gurganus
J. A. Creech	A. M. Hicks
F. M. Moss	R. A. Redfern
G. G. Tart	

ALEXANDER   BASS   BRAWLEY

CONN   GILCHRIST   HUFFMAN   KING

McLELLAN   MUNCH   POPLIN   SUTHER

E. F. THOMAS   H. C. THOMAS   USHER   WYCHE

ALPHA CHI SIGMA

Founded at the University of Wisconsin, 1902

Colors: Prussian Blue and Crome Yellow   *Flower:* Red Carnation

Publication: The Hexagon

Rho Chapter
Established 1912

Fratres in Facultate

Dr. F. P. Venable   Dr. J. T. Dobbins
Dr. J. M. Bell   Dr. H. D. Crockford
Dr. A. S. Wheeler   Dr. F. K. Cameron
Dr. F. C. Vilbrandt   Dr. F. H. Edmister
Dr. R. W. Bost

Fratres in Universitate

Class of 1930
R. E. Bass
D. J. Brawley

Class of 1931
A. L. Alexander   R. L. Poplin
G. H. McCormic   Frank Thomas
R. H. Munch   H. C. Thomas
E. H. Wyche

Class of 1932
Earle O. Bryant   M. M. Matthews
P. S. Gilchrist, Jr.   J. Allan Suther
P. C. Usher

Graduates
R. F. Abernethy   T. L. King
Miller W. Conn   H. A. Ljung
E. W. Constable   W. J. Mattox
D. R. Ergle   C. R. McLellan
E. S. Gilbreath   Haywood Parker
E. E. Huffman   J. H. Sanders
J. B. Joyner   W. W. Williams

BANNER   CARLISLE   CLINARD   COOPER   DRESSLAR

FARRELL   FOLLIN   GLENN   GORHAM   HENDERSON

HINES   JAMESON   LYNCH   McCOTTER   MERRITT

MILLS   PATTERSON   PLEASANTS   J.C.SHELTON   T.M. SHELTON

SICKLES   SLATER   STULTZ   WADDILL   WATKINS

ALPHA KAPPA PSI
Founded at New York University, 1904

Colors: Blue and Gold

Publication: Alpha Kappa Psi Diary

Alpha Tau Chapter
Established 1925

Fratres in Facultate

DUDLEY DEWITT CARROLL
CLAUDIUS TEMPLE MURCHISON
ERLE EWERT PEACOCK

HARRY ALBERT HARING
ROBERT ALLEN MCPHEETERS
COLLIER BRYSON SPARGER

Fratres in Universitate
Class of 1930

C. W. BANNER
M. G. FOLLIN
R. C. MERRITT
W. L. CARLISLE

D. C. MCCOTTER
J. C. SHELTON
L. C. STEWART, JR.
E. L. WADDILL

Class of 1931

E. G. HINES
C. B. MACKETHAN
A. S. WATKINS

C. E. PLEASANTS
H. N. PATTERSON

Pledges

A. B. CARR
J. P. COOPER
W. M. CROUCH
O. W. DRESSLAR
ROBERT FARRELL
M. S. GLENN
H. J. STULTZ
JOHN CLINARD

W. I. HENDERSON
HARLAN JAMESON
J. S. GORHAM, JR.
S. A. LYNCH, JR.
B. S. MILLS, JR.
T. M. SHELTON, JR.
J. S. SLATER
A. D. SICKLES

AARON   BARBER   BRAINARD   CONLEY

EDWARDS   FERGUSON   H.D.HARRIS   B.W.HARRIS,JR.   HIGDON

LASSITER   MENDENHALL   MOUNT   PREVOST   REDDING

ROACH   THOMPSON   WILEY   WINECOFF   ZACKARY

DELTA SIGMA PI

Founded at New York University, 1907

Colors: Old Gold and Royal Purple   *Flower:* Red Rose

Publication: The Delta Sig

Alpha Lambda Chapter
Established 1925

Fratres in Facultate

G. T. SCHWENNING	E. W. ZIMMERMAN
M. D. TAYLOR	J. M. LEAR
H. D. WOLF	M. S. HEATH
J. G. EVANS	

Fratres in Urbe

A. A. PERKINS
THERA E. HINSON

Fratres in Universitate

Class of 1930

H. I. AARON	W. L. HIGDON, JR.
B. W. HARRIS, JR.	J. C. REDDING
E. E. MENDENHALL, JR.	W. H. PREVOST.
G. C. WINECOFF	G. L. CONLEY
H. G. BRAINARD	M. D. LASSITER
S. R. WILEY	

Class of 1931

G. P. BOURDELOT	F. J. FERGUSON
A. A. MOUNT	J. F. PARROT
W. C. THOMPSON	H. D. HARRIS
G. H. ROACH	

Class of 1932

R. N. BARBER
C. R. ZACHARY
W. W. EDWARDS
J. P. SHERRILL

Graduates

Y. M. SMITH
D. F. MARTIN

PHI BETA KAPPA

Founded at the College of William and Mary, 1776

Alpha Chapter of North Carolina

GORDON GRAY ....:.*President*

WILLIAM JACKSON ADAMS, JR. ....*Vice-President*

THOMAS JAMES WILSON, JR. ....*Corresponding Secretary and Treasurer*

Student Members

William Jackson Adams, Jr.
Charles Whitlock Banner, Jr.
Marcus Battle Braswell
Travis Taylor Brown
Clarence Coleman Cates
Ralph Stokes Collins
William Rodolph Curtis
Charles Patterson Graham
Robert Lee Graham, Jr.
Gordon Gray
Robert McDonald Gray, Jr.
Ralph Cordell Greene
Robert Alexander Hovis

Frank Short Howell
Franklin Banks Kuykendal, Jr.
John Albert Lang
John Baker Lewis
Rufus Reid Little
George Attmore Long
John Milton McNeil
Charles Staples Mangum, Jr.
William Leak Marshall, Jr.
James Eric Merritt
Robert Long Murphey
Samuel Eugene Pace
Haywood Parker, Jr.

Manning Mason Pattillo
Louis Jefferson Ring
Charles Francis Rouse
Allen Kendrick Smith
Thomas Carlyle Smith, Jr.
Cecil Grady Taylor
Francis Rogers Toms
Wingate Edgerton Underhill
Henrietta Underwood
Charles Edward Waddell, Jr.
Herbert Christy Wall
Robert Hoke Webb
Robert Lyles Zealy

Members in the City

Eleanor Elliott Carroll
Columbia
Mary Louisa Cobb
North Carolina
Louis Graves
North Carolina
Barbara Henderson
North Carolina
Alma Holland
North Carolina
Katherine Jocher
Goucher

Guion Griffis Johnson
North Carolina
Estelle Edith Lawson
North Carolina
Romana Galloway Mackie
North Carolina
Eleanor Schmidt Mosher
North Carolina
Luther James Phipps
North Carolina

Charles Edwin Ray, Jr.
North Carolina
Gertrude Samuels
North Carolina
Rosalie Thrall
North Carolina
Calvert Rogers Toy
North Carolina
Hazel Terry Trimble
North Carolina
Louise Manning Venable
North Carolina

Members in the Faculty

N. B. Adams, Ph.D.
Washington and Lee

H. G. Baity, Sc.D.
North Carolina

S. B. Barnes, A.B.
Columbia

C. D. Beers, Ph.D.
North Carolina

L. J. Bell, Jr., A.B.
North Carolina

W. R. Berryhill, A.B., M.D.
North Carolina

R. S. Boggs, Ph.B.
Chicago

R. P. Bond, Ph.D.
Vanderbilt

F. F. Bradshaw, M.A.
North Carolina

G. M. Braune, C.E.
Washington and Lee

K. J. Brown, Ph.D.
Dickinson

R. M. Brown, Ph.D.
North Carolina

E. T. Browne, Ph.D.
Virginia

J. B. Bullitt, A.M., M.D.
Washington and Lee

R. C. Bullock, A.M.
North Carolina

W. E. Caldwell, Ph.D.
Cornell

E. A. Cameron, A.B.Educ.
North Carolina

H. W. Chase, Ph.D., LL.D.
Dartmouth

R. E. Coker, Ph.D.
North Carolina

W. C. Coker, Ph.D.
Johns Hopkins

H. W. Crane, Ph.D.
Michigan

W. M. Dey, Ph.D.
Virginia

S. A. Emery, Ph.D.
Cornell

F. P. Graham, M.A.
North Carolina

F. M. Green, Ph.D.
North Carolina

M. H. Griffin, Ph.D.
Georgia

E. R. Groves, A.B., B.D.
Dartmouth

J. M. Gwynn, A.M.
North Carolina

J. G. deR. Hamilton, Ph.D.
William and Mary

J. P. Harland, Ph.D.
Princeton

G. A. Harrer, Ph.D.
Princeton

Clarence Heer, Ph.D.
Rochester

A. Henderson, Ph.D., LL.D.,
D.C.L.
North Carolina

U. T. Holmes, Ph.D.
Pennsylvania

R. B. House, A.M.
North Carolina

George Howe, Ph.D
Princeton

E. C. Hunter, A.B.Educ.
North Carolina

A. C. Jennings, A.B.
North Carolina

H. M. Jones, M.A.
Wisconsin

A. K. King, A.M.
North Carolina

E. W. Knight, Ph.D.
Duke

J. W. Lasley, Jr., Ph.D.
North Carolina

J. B. Linker, Ph.D.
North Carolina

J. C. Lyons, Ph.D.
William and Mary

G. R. MacCarthy, Ph.D.
North Carolina

A. C. McIntosh, A.M., LL.D.
Davidson

E. L. Mackie, Ph.D.
North Carolina

R. S. Matthews, A.B.
North Carolina

T. P. Noe, S.B.
North Carolina

W. W. Pierson, Jr., Ph.D.
Alabama

R. R. Potter, Ph.D.
North Carolina

W. F. Prouty, Ph.D.
Johns Hopkins

W. C. Salley, A.B.
Alabama

Thorndike Saville, C.E., M.S.
Dartmouth

H. E. Spivey, A.B.
North Carolina

E. D. Strong, M.A.
Grinnell

J. H. Swartz, Ph.D.
Johns Hopkins

G. C. Taylor, Ph.D.
South Carolina

M. R. Trabue, Ph.D.
Northwestern

R. B. Vance, Ph.D.
North Carolina

F. P. Venable, Ph.D.
North Carolina

F. C. Vilbrandt, Ph.D.
Ohio State

P. W. Wager, Ph.D.
Hobart

H. M. Wagstaff, Ph.D.
Johns Hopkins

N. W. Walker, A.B., Ed.M.
North Carolina

A. S. Wheeler, Ph.D.
Beloit

L. R. Wilson, Ph.D.
North Carolina

T. J. Wilson, Jr., Ph.D.
North Carolina

T. J. Wilson, III, D.Phil.
North Carolina

E. J. Woodhouse, B.A., LL.B.
Randolph-Macon

L. B. Wright, Ph.D.
North Carolina

ALEXANDER   BURNETT   DRAKE   HEDGPETH   KUYKENDAL

LEAR   THOMPSON   TOMS   WHITE

PHI ZETA NU
Established 1919

Colors: Red and Green

Fratres in Facultate
JOHN E. LEAR   ELMER G. HOEFER
GEORGE W. SMITH

Fratres in Universitate
Class of 1930

JOHN J. ALEXANDER	T. V. HEDGPETH
WILLIAM C. BURNETT	C. MERRITT LEAR
FRANCIS E. DRAKE	FRANCIS R. TOMS
F. B. KUYKENDAL, JR.	WILLIAM B. WHITE

Class of 1931
GEORGE D. THOMPSON

BOBBITT   HEDGEPETH   KUYKENDAL

TOMS   UNDERHILL   WADDELL   WHITE

TAU BETA PI
Founded at Lehigh University, 1885

Colors: Brown and White   Publication: The Bent

Beta Chapter of North Carolina

W. E. Bobbitt _____President
F. R. Toms_____Secretary
F. B. Kuykendal_____ _____Treasurer

Student Members

W. E. Underhill   C. E. Waddell
T. V. Hedgpeth   W. B. White

Graduate

A. B. Uzzle, Jr.

Faculty Members

Dean G. M. Braune   T. F. Hickerson   R. M. Trimble
H. G. Baity   E. G. Hoefer   N. P. Bailey
T. P. Noe   E. W. Winkler   G. W. Smith

ALBRIGHT   CARR   FISHER   HARRIS   HAYWOOD

HOBGOOD   SPEIGHT   WILKINSON   WILLIAMS

TAU KAPPA ALPHA

Founded at Indianapolis, 1908

Colors: Dark and Light Purple   *Publication*: The Speaker of Tau Kappa Alpha

Fratres in Facultate

C. E. McIntosh	W. T. Couch
W. S. Branard	C. W. Beer
F. F. Bradshaw	F. P. Graham
Albert Coates	R. B. House

Fratres in Urbe

L. V. Huggins   James Phipps
H. N. Brown, III

Fratres in Universitate

R. M. Albright	J. C. Harris	J. M. Mewborn
G. P. Carr	E. L. Haywood	W. W. Speight
O. B. Eaton	H. H. Hobgood	J. C. Williams
R. B. Fisher	J. B. Lewis	J. A. Wilkinson

WIGUE AND MASQUE

WEX MALONE ⎯⎯⎯⎯⎯⎯⎯⎯⎯⎯⎯⎯⎯⎯⎯⎯⎯⎯⎯⎯⎯⎯*President*

GEORGE RACE ⎯⎯⎯⎯⎯⎯⎯⎯⎯⎯⎯⎯⎯⎯⎯⎯⎯⎯⎯*Vice-President*

JACK KIRKPATRICK ⎯⎯⎯⎯⎯⎯⎯⎯⎯⎯⎯⎯⎯⎯⎯⎯*Secretary*

CRAIG SHELTON ⎯⎯⎯⎯⎯⎯⎯⎯⎯⎯⎯⎯⎯⎯⎯⎯⎯⎯⎯*Treasurer*

Faculty Members

U. T. HOLMES
T. S. McCORKLE
OTTO STUHLMAN

Student Members

DAVE AVNER	PHOEBE HARDING
ELIZABETH BARBER	FRANK HOWELL
BLOCK BRYSON	CLIFF KIEM
FRED BYERLY	ART LITTLE
BETH COLLEY	HELEN McKAY
VERNON COWPER	TOM ROLLINS
KELSO CURRIE	PAUL SCURLOCK
FRED DICK	ART SICKLES
CELESTE EDGERTON	JAMES TURNER
D. L. ENGLISH	THOMAS UZZELL
RICHARD FENKER	DICK WALSER
MAURINE FORESTER	JACK WHITE
HARRY GALLAND	DON WOOD

THE COOP

Officers

GENE WELLS ....President
DUSTY SKINNER ....Secretary and Treasurer
GEORGE SANDERS ....Manager

Members

"Ichabod" Ruffin
"Felix the Cat" Huger
"Big Time" Dick
"Kate" Graham
"Kitty" Wood
"Chink" Davis
"Jack" Paschau
"Henry" Benoit
"Yon" Yemson
"Mole Eye" Rhett
"Sentimental" Brown
"John" Clinard
"Pat" Patterson
"Fred" Carr
"Judy" Palmore
"Joe" Carpenter
"Bill" Adams
"Student" Ward
"Mel" Lindsay
"Crude" Hudson
"Lawyer" Adams
"Sissy" Sanders
"Strud" Nash
"Rufe" Little

"Big Red" Wily
"Unconscious" Bagby
"Flat Tire" Ford
"Doggie" Dunn
"Sam" Peace
"Gene" Wells
"Kike" Henderson
"Steve" Millender
"Ugene" Hines
"John" Park
"Branch" Carr
"Hot Pants" Toms
"Chas." Rollins
"Harry" Finch
"John" Ferebee
"Slow" Henderson
"Zeke" Cozart
"Dusty" Skinner
"Art" Kaufman
"Chief" Ramsay
"Ma" Parsley
"Fanny" Houston
"Jabber" Ashcraft
"Jerrie" Doughtie

"Bill" Marshall

THE CABIN

CHARLIE SHANNON ....*President*
ALEX DALEY ....*Secretary*
VAL HEDGPETH ....*Manager*

Members

"Archie" Allen
"Billy" Atkinson
"Tom" Bennett
"Billy" Bryan
"Fred" Brickman
"Bill" Bridgers
"Swift" Boatwright
"Billy" Cheatham
"W. G." Brown
"Chap" Crawford
"Red" Constantine
"John Phil" Cooper
"Bob" Dewey
"Alex" Daley
"Jack" Dunavant
"Joe" Eagles
"Pace" Fuller
"Bob" Graham
"Donald" Graham
"B. K." Grier
"Paul" Gilbert
"George" Hamer
"Ped" Hamer
"Val" Hedgpeth
"Frank" Howell
"George" Houston
"Buddy" Hubbard

"George" Heinitsh
"Phil" Jackson
"Larry" Johnson
"Link" Kesler
"John" London
"Lonnie" London
"'Onrie" London
"Commodore" Miller
"D. C." McCotter
"Dave" Nims
"Mull-Head" Parker
"Cooper" Person
"T. H." Redding
"Tally" Redfern
"Vance" Rollins
"Vic" Ruehl
"George" Rosemond
"Frank" Spruill
"Bill" Sharpe
"Charlie" Shannon
"Billy" Satterfield
"C. C." Sikes
"Emil" Shaffner
"Henry" Stultz
"Herbert" Taylor
"Charlie" Woodward
"Rudy" Waddill

"Dick" Winborne

MINOTAURS

George Lewis Bagby...M. W. H.

Charles C. Skinner...M. W. U.

William Dunn, Jr...B. T.

George Lee Race...B. M. B.

Herbert Best...H. D. K. D.

EDMUND STRUDWICK NASH

GEORGE DEWEY THOMPSON

EDGAR COOPER PERSON

CHARLES GWYN CHATHAM

EDWARD RUSSELL LIPSCOMB

EDWARD RYAN HAMER

MEADE HOMER WILLIS

CHARLES ELLIN FORD

MANDEVILLE A. WEBB

JOHN ALSEY PARK

THOMAS WILLIS ALEXANDER

LOUIS CHERRY SKINNER

JOEL JENKINS HUTCHINSON

LYNN WILDER

THOMAS BARBER FOLLIN

WILLIAM T. MYERS

GEORGE WATERHOUSE

WILLIAM ASHBY BRIDGERS

Huts

ROUSE

PRICE

PALMORE

TOMS

REDFERN

MARSHALL

ALLEN

GRAY, G.

GRAY, B.

CRAIG

ORDER OF THE SHEIKS

GAVIN H. DORTCH .... *S.*

JOE C. EAGLES .... *V. S.*

PETER B. RUFFIN .... *K.*

G. VERNON COWPER	W. H. YARBOROUGH, JR.
MCDONALD GRAY	HENRY B. WEBB
CHARLES P. GRAHAM	SAMUEL MCCONNELL, JR.
NELSON WOODSON	HENRY C. HOUSE
JUNIUS G. ADAMS	J. WORTH MCALISTER
CHARLES E. WADDELL	THOMAS L. PARSONS
JULIAN B. FENNER	J. HOLMES DAVIS, JR.
CHARLES L. SMITH, JR.	EDWARD F. YARBOROUGH
J. FLEMING WILY, JR.	FRED JONES, JR.
H. DAIL HOLDERNESS	GEORGE L. JONES
EUGENE WELLS	HENRY L. ANDERSON
RICHARD WINBORN	MARION GLENN
GEORGE W. SANDERS	PETER S. GILCHRIST
WILLIAM S. KOENIG	HUBERT H. O'DONNELL
R. MAYNE ALBRIGHT	HARRY C. FINCH
JOHN VAN LINDLEY	WILLIAM R. SATTERFIELD
GEORGE P. MOODY	A. REID PERKINS, JR.

FRANK A. COLE, JR.

Thomas A. Uzzell, Jr.	Beta Theta Pi
A. Baron Holmes	Sigma Alpha Epsilon
Herman Schnell	Delta Psi
Marion Follin, Jr.	Beta Theta Pi
Homer L. Lyon, Jr.	Zeta Psi
Frederick L. Carr	Sigma Nu
Edmund L. Waddill	Delta Tau Delta
Thomas Craig	Delta Kappa Epsilon
Lindsay C. Plumly	Beta Theta Pi
John C. Grainger	Delta Psi
James S. Hudson	Sigma Alpha Epsilon
Egbert L. Haywood	Chi Phi
Charles Woodward	Alpha Tau Omega
Henry House	Kappa Alpha
Willis Henderson	Sigma Nu
Chauncey Royster	Sigma Chi
Harry Shaner	Pi Kappa Alpha
Emil N. Shaffner	Delta Tau Delta
Kenneth A. Gay	Delta Psi
William F. Draper	Beta Theta Pi
Joe H. Carpenter	Sigma Alpha Epsilon
Sydney L. Lea	Delta Psi
Edward K. Graham	Zeta Psi
John D. Branch	Chi Phi
B. T. Grier	Alpha Tau Omega
Sam T. Peace	Kappa Alpha
L. Branch Carr	Sigma Nu
Thomas Shelton, Jr.	Sigma Chi
George Ward Thompson	Pi Kappa Alpha
Charles Rollins	Delta Tau Delta
Reid Brawley	Alpha Tau Omega

J. G. deRoulhac Hamilton
Francis Foster Bradshaw
William Terry Couch
Ernest Lloyd Mackie
John Maryon Saunders
William J. Adams, Jr.
John Huske Anderson, Jr.
Travis Taylor Brown
Harry J. Galland
John Frazier Glenn
Robert Lee Graham
Glenn Parran Holder
John H. Mebane
David A. Nims
Joe Jones

Douglas Laten Potter
James Jerry Slade
Robert Lyles Zealy
Mayne Albright
Herbert T. Browne
Stanley Ellis Crew
Joseph Colin Eagles
Gordon Gray
Oscar W. Dresslar
Harry Clinton Finch
Richard M. Fenker
Herbert Hechenbleikner
Jack Schneider

Faculty Members

Francis Foster Bradshaw
Albert Coates
Frank Porter Graham
J. Minor Gwynn
Clarence A. Hibbard
A. C. Howell
A. A. Perkins
William M. Saunders
J. F. Steiner

Students

C. W. Banner
A. E. Bavacqua
A. J. Buttitta
T. T. Brown
W. C. Dunn
H. A. Estep
H. J. Galland
Calvin Graves
Harry Grossman

E. R. Hamer
L. T. Hammond
G. P. Holder
K. L. Kjellesvig
Pedro Kjellesvig
J. A. Lang
T. A. Libbus
B. C. Moore
Alfredo Nazareno
B. M. Parker
J. B. Pittana
Douglas Potter
T. B. Rector
J. J. Slade
A. J. Thomas
J. C. Williams
F. V. Zappa
R. L. Zealy

ORDER OF THE GOLDEN FLEECE

Honorary Members

HENRY HORACE WILLIAMS   HARRY WOODBURN CHASE

Faculty Members

CHARLES THOMAS WOOLEN   ERNEST LLOYD MACKIE
FRANK PORTER GRAHAM   ALBERT COATES
EDGAR RALPH RANKIN   JOE BURTON LINKER
FRANCIS FOSTER BRADSHAW   JEFFERSON CARNEY BYNUM
ROBERT BURTON HOUSE   CORYDON PERRY SPRUILL
HERMAN GLENN BAITY   EDWARD ALEXANDER CAMERON
WILLIAM TERRY COUCH   JOSEPH MARYON SAUNDERS

Graduate Students

ROBERT MCDONALD GRAY   JOHN FRAZIER GLENN, JR.
CHARLES EDWARD WADDELL, JR.   KILLIAN BARWICK

Active Argonauts

JUNIUS GREENE ADAMS, JR.   RALPH CORDELL GREENE
TRAVIS TAYLOR BROWN   JOHN MIDDLETON HENDERSON
RAY SIMPSON FARRIS   GLENN PARRAN HOLDER
HARRY JOSEPH GALLAND   JAMES MAUS
GORDON GRAY   JAMES WILLIAM WILLIAMS

Order of the Grail

Officers

Marion Follin, Jr...Del.
Edward R. Hamer...Sc.
Ralph C. Greene..Ex.
R. M. Albright..Asst.-Ex.

Faculty Members

Horace Williams   William S. Bernard

Members

Robert Mayne Albright, Jr.
John H. Anderson
Killian Barwick
Travis Taylor Brown
Edward Alexander Cameron
Walter D. Creech
Joseph Colin Eagles
Ray Simpson Farris
Marion G. Follin, Jr.
Harry Joseph Galland
John Frazier Glenn
Robert McDonald Gray
Ralph C. Greene
Edward R. Hamer
John Middleton Henderson

Henry C. House
John Desmond Idol
Joseph Piper Jones
Henry Johnston, Jr.
Isaac H. Manning, Jr.
George Dawson McDaniel
David Anderson Nims
Robert Aubrey Parsley
Henry N. Patterson
Aubrey A. Perkins
Douglas M. Potter
John Gary Slater
James Allen Williams
James William Williams
Robert Lyles Zealy

GORGON'S HEAD

Officers

DAVID JENKINS CRAIG, JR._____*President*

JULIAN IVANHOE PALMORE _____*Secretary*

THOMAS BENJAMIN BENNETT, JR. _____*Treasurer*

Faculty Members

LOUIS GRAVES
CHARLES THOMAS WOOLEN
JOHN MANNING BOOKER
WILLIAM MORTON DEY
JAMES BELL BULLIT
ROBERT DIGGS WIMBERLY CONNOR
WILLIAM DEBERNIERE MCNIDER
CLARENCE ADDISON HIBBARD

CLAUDIUS TEMPLE MURCHISON
WILLIAM DOUGLAS MACMILLAN
KENNER CHAPMAN FRASER
ROLAND PRINCE MCCLAMROCK
NICHOLAS BARNEY ADAMS
URBAN TIGNER HOLMES
JAMES RUEY PATRICK
CHARLES TILFORD MCCORMICK

WILLIAM RICHARSON ABBOTT

Members

JUNIUS GREENE ADAMS, JR.
JOHN DAVID BULLOCK, JR.
JOHN HUSKE ANDERSON
THOMAS CARLISLE SMITH, JR.
ALEXANDER BARON HOLMES
WILLIAM DAVID POPE SHARPE, JR.
WILLIAM PACE FULLER
ARCHIE TURNER ALLEN

DAVID JENKINS CRAIG, JR.
JULIAN IVANHOE PALMORE
THOMAS BENJAMIN BENNETT, JR.
JOHN THOMAS CRAIG
WILLIAM CHURCHILL CHEATHAM
EDGAR COOPER PERSON, JR.
FRANCIS OGDEN PARKER
CHAUNCEY LAKE ROYSTER

HAYWOOD DAIL HOLDERNESS

RULERS

SUBJECTS

VANITY
FAIR

William Makepeace Thackeray

THACKERAY

What can be prettier than an image of Love on his knees before Beauty?

—VANITY FAIR.

Miss Dorothy Harper

Miss Virginia Dunklee

MISS ELIZABETH HANES

MISS MARIAN CLARKE

MISS SARAH LUMMUS

Miss Alice Caldwell

Miss Rebecca Daniels

MISS LUCY FURMAN

MISS HARRIET WYNNE

MISS DOROTHY WELBORN

THE
DANCE

Lord Byron

BYRON

On with the dance!
Let joy be unconfined.
No sleep till morn
When youth and pleasure meet.
— CHILDE HAROLD'S PILGRIMAGE.

EXECUTIVE COMMITTEE
OF THE GERMAN CLUB

YARBOROUGH   BROWN   RACE CHAIRMAN   PALMORE   BULLUCK

GRAY   ALBRIGHT   DUNN   SANDERS

Executive Committee of the German Club

GEORGE RACE——Chairman

Julian Palmore	John Bulluck
Will Yarborough	Travis Brown
Gordon Gray	Mayne Albright
George Saunders	Bill Dunn

GEORGE RACE, *President*   MISS ELIZABETH HANES

JULIAN PALMORE, *Vice-President*   MISS KITTY BODDIE

WM. YARBOROUGH, *Secy.-Treas.*   MISS RUTH DAVIS

German Club

BERT HAYWOOD, *Leader*   MISS DOROTHY HARPER

JULIAN PALMORE   MISS KITTY BODDIE

CRAIG SHELTON   MISS ELIZABETH SNYDER

Fall German

STEPHEN MILLENDER, *Leader*   MISS FRANCES MOORE

ARTHUR SICKLES   MISS ELIZABETH BARBER

BARRON GRIER   MISS PAULINE WEBB

Mid-Winter German

[336]

FLEMING WILY, *Leader*   MISS JANE ROGERS

WILLIAM MARSHALL   MISS DORA LITTLE

GEORGE RACE   MISS ELIZABETH HANES

Gimghoul Ball

LARRY JOHNSON, *Leader*   MISS JERRY LEE

WARD THOMPSON   MISS ANNETTA MACLEAN

LYNN WILDER   MISS NANCY FISH

Sophomore Hop

WILLIS HENDERSON, *Leader*   MISS ALICE HOUSTON QUARLES

MARION COWPER   MISS STEPHANIE BRAGAW

GREGORY PEELER   MISS CHRISTINE HUDSON

Junior Prom

JOHN GILLESPIE, *Leader*   MISS ELIZABETH ADAMS

PETER GILCHRIST   MISS SOPHIA CLIFTON

HENRY STULTZ   MISS RUTH BOGER

Sophomore Prom

RALPH GREENE, *Leader*   MISS ALICE ELIZABETH FREEZE

ROBERT MERRITT   MISS MARY LOU VENTERS

JULIAN FENNER   MISS MARIE ANDERSON

Senior Ball

· HENRY HOUSE, *Leader*   MISS ELIZABETH ALLEN

HERBERT NELSON   MISS FRANCES STRATTON

JACK LINDLEY   MISS ELIZABETH HANES

Junior Ball

COMMENCEMENT MARSHALS

ROYSTER

WOODARD
CHIEF

HAMER

THOMPSON

FARRELL

MANNING

LINDSAY

GILBERT

COMMENCEMENT BALL MANAGERS

LEONARD HOLE
CHIEF

MAURINE FORESTER

TOM HUNTER

DOROTHY KLUTZ

JACK CALHOUN

CATHERINE FEE

ARCHIE ALLEN

ANNETTE TUCKER

WILLIAM ADAMS

HENRIETTA WHISNANT

CHARLES PRICE

DORA LITTLE

PHILLIP JACKSON

MARY NEAL WILKINS

ALLEN BOREN

ELIZABETH BOWIE

[344]

ATHLETICS

Alexander the Great

ALEXANDER THE GREAT

There is joy in the combat, and in the winning of it.

Coach ROBERT FETZER
Director of Athletics

IN APPRECIATION

DURING the ten years that Coach "Bob," as he is more popularly
known, has been at Carolina, athletics have progressed by leaps
and bounds. During this time he has made himself, as well as the
University, well known in athletic circles.

In track, the sport in which Coach 'Bob" seems to specialize, for
the past ten years the Tar Heel teams have been State champions
for each year of the ten, Southern Conference champions once, and
National 4-mile relay champions.

The Carolinians have been equally successful in basketball, football, and all other sports under the regime of Mr. Fetzer. He has
undoubtedly been the backbone of athletics, and his directorship can
be only praised.

The men on the teams all honor and respect him, and co-operate
to the fullest extent with him. The success of the teams is probably
due to this cause, and will continue as long as he is head of athletics.
The title of "Dean of Southern Track" has been conveyed upon him
by numerous sports writers, and he is known and respected by his
fellow coaches throughout the South.

Enough tribute cannot be paid to this man who has done so much
for athletics at Carolina, but in appreciation of his work and influence
in Southern athletics we dedicate the Sports Section to Mr. Robert
Fetzer, "Coach Bob."

1929
CAPTAIN
FARRIS

FOOTBALL

1930
CAPTAIN
NASH

1929 FOOTBALL SQUAD

FOOTBALL 1929

Head Coach............."Chuck" Collins

Assistant Coach............"Bill" Cerney

Assistant Coach ...."Bob" Fetzer

Trainer......................P. H. Quinlan

Captain ....Ray Farris

Manager ....Dave Craig

"Chuck" Collins

"Dave" Craig

The Schedule

Sept. 28—Wake Forest	0	Carolina	48
Oct. 5—Maryland	0	Carolina	43
Oct. 12—Georgia Tech	7	Carolina	18
Oct. 19—Georgia	19	Carolina	12
Oct. 26—V. P. I.	13	Carolina	38
Nov. 2—N. C. State	0	Carolina	32
Nov. 9—South Carolina	0	Carolina	40
Nov. 16—Davidson	7	Carolina	26
Nov. 28—Virginia	7	Carolina	41
Dec. 7—Duke University	7	Carolina	48

Summary

Games won....................9   Games lost....................1

Third in the Southern Conference. Second in National high scores.

Total points..................846   Total opponents..............60

"Bill" Cerney

"Bob" Fetzer

P. H. Quinlan

Nash, back

Holt, end

Adkins, tackle

Branch being stopped by Virginia man after long gain

Spaulding starts through the line—U. N. C. vs. V. P. I.

Football

Although the Tar Heel eleven faced one of the hardest ten game schedules in the South at the opening of the 1929 season, they started off their program with the spectacular defeat of the Wake Forest eleven and wound up their schedule by taking the Blue Devils in tow by one of the largest wins ever made against the Durham institution to finish the season with 9 wins and 1 defeat. Carolina set a new high scoring team average of 34.6 points to place second among the national high scorers, and to have one man given honorable mention for a mythical All-American team and three placed on All-Southern picks. In addition to victories over Wake Forest and Duke, Carolina can record wins over last year's national champions, Georgia Tech, and Maryland, Virginia, V. P. I., South Carolina, N. C. State, and Davidson. The only mar of the entire season came in one quarter of the University of Georgia game in Kenan Stadium which resulted in a 19 to 12 victory for the Bulldogs, conquerors of the Yale Bulldog, 15 to 0.

Farris, guard

Ward, back

Branch, back

Fysal, guard

YACKETY YACK

Magner, back

Koenig, tackle

Erickson, back

Captain Ray Farris led the Tar Heels with individual honors when he was given honorable mention for a mythical All-American eleven and was unanimously chosen on the All-Southern first team. In addition to this, the Varsity placed two men on the second team picked by several prominent news syndicates. Johnnie Branch, diminutive quarter, and Jim Magner, smashing fleetfooted half, were the other two Tar Heel representatives. Honorable mention was given to many of the Tar Heels for positions on the All-Southern picks. Among these were Capt.-elect Strud Nash, halfback; Ned Lipscomb, center; Pot Adkins, tackle; Don Holt, end; Yank Spaulding, fullback; Jimmy Ward, half; and Bill Koenig, tackle.

Eight of the Tar Heels represented Carolina on the mythical All-State eleven, and in several selections the whole team was composed of Carolina men.

Carolina 48 vs. Wake Forest 0

The 48 to 0 win over Wake Forest in Kenan Stadium clearly showed the offensive power of the Varsity at the beginning of the season.

Nash off for a gain against Georgia

Branch returns a kickoff against Duke

Spaulding, back   Lipscomb, center   Fenner, end   House, back

[351]

Hudson, guard

Slusser, back

Gilbreath, center

Ward breaks through tackle against Georgia for a nice gain

Virginia man starting around end at the Thanksgiving Day game

Carolina 43 vs. Maryland 0

Continuing their winning stride the Tar Heels tumbled Maryland for the second year in a row by turning in the largest Old Liner defeat ever made by the Tar Heel eleven in a onesided 43 to 0 clash at College Park, Maryland. The Varsity's backs literally ran wild in the last few minutes of play to such an extent that one could almost truthfully assert that Collins had a "hundred backs" at his disposal.

Carolina 18 vs. Georgia Tech 7

In this annual game with Georgia Tech, Carolina showed her worth more clearly than ever by the manner in which the team conquered the Techman, 18 to 7. The outstanding playing of the entire Carolina eleven, and the spectacular return of punts by the diminutive Johnnie Branch featured the Tar Heel win over the Yellow Jackets in Atlanta. Nearly 500 students accompanied the team to Atlanta.

Carolina 12 vs. U. of Georgia 19

The national aspirations of the U. N. C. sport world fell with the Georgia victory in Kenan Stadium, 19 to 12. The game was hard fought throughout and was not won until the last whistle.

Eskew, guard   Dortch, tackle   Parsley, end   Harden, back

Thompson, tackle

Wyrick, back

McIver, guard

Carolina 38 vs. V. P. I. 13

The Virginia Poly Institute journied down from Blacksburg to give the Tar Heels a chance to avenge last year's one-point defeat by a 38-13 score. The Carolina team was superior in every phase of the game.

Carolina 32 vs. N. C. State 0

Vengeance was also loosed upon the N. C. State Wolfpack by the tune of 32-0 when the Tar Heel attacked them in Kenan Stadium. Nearly 40 of the Tar Heels saw action in this game where much new material was tested.

Carolina 40 vs. S. Car. 0

In one of the most talked about games of the season, "the Battle of the Carolinas," the Tar Heels easily clipped the Gamecocks' wings, 40 to 0, before a homecoming crowd in Columbia. The North Carolina offense was too much for the South Carolinians.

Carolina 26 vs. Davidson 7

The Davidson Wildcats bared their fangs before the onrush of the Tar Heel eleven and held them to a mere 26-7 win when they met at Davidson.

The start of a gain against Duke

Spaulding kicks a goal for Carolina

Jackson, back

Nelson, end

Brown, end

Maus, back

YACKE

Tabb, end   Harper, tackle   Crew, guard   Redfern, back

Georgia scores a goal against Carolina

State starts to pass in U. N. C. game in Kenan Stadium

Carolina 41 vs. Virginia 7

In the annual turkey day classic between the Universities of North Carolina and Virginia at the Hill, the Carolinians trounced the friendly Cavaliers by the largest Tar Heel victory ever turned in over a Virginia eleven, 41 to 7. Nearly 30,000 spectators saw the Tar Heel backs show spectacular form on offense and defense while the Virginians found the forward line to be virtually a "stonewall." Sloan, Virginia back, created a sensation when he ran 95 yards from kick-off for the only Virginia score. This incidentally, was the longest run ever made in Kenan Stadium. Spaulding, N. C. fullback, and Capt. Farris of N. C., were high lights in the game, especially on the defense.

Carolina 48 vs. Duke 7

The Tar Heels finished their hard 10 game schedule with one of the largest Duke defeats they had ever made, 48 to 7, when they met in the new Duke Stadium. The entire Tar Heel eleven functioned as one in this final game of the season. Strud Nash was high score with three touchdowns.

Nash breaks loose against Georgia   Duke man starting an off-tackle play

[354]

YACKETY YACK

1930
CAPTAIN
HARPER

BASKETBALL

1931
CAPTAIN
MARPET

[355]

1930 BASKETBALL SQUAD

BASKETBALL 1930

Coach ....Jim Ashmore

Honorary Captain........"Puny" Harper

Manager ....Loy Thompson

Coach Ashmore   **Manager Thompson**

The Schedule

January 11—Davidson 22	Carolina....................20
January 14—Guilford 20	Carolina....................49
January 16—Washington and Lee 39	Carolina....................24
January 21—Charlotte Monograms 19	Carolina....................23
January 25—Wake Forest 18	Carolina....................49
January 28—N. C. State 25	Carolina....................27
February 1—Duke University 86	Carolina....................14
February 5—V. P. I. 21	Carolina....................80
February 6—Washington and Lee.........27	Carolina....................17
February 7—Virginia 87	Carolina....................40
February 8—Maryland 86	Carolina....................88
February 11—N. C. State 28	Carolina....................26
February 12—Loyola 26	Carolina....................25
February 15—Duke 87	Carolina....................86
February 18—Wake Forest 15	Carolina....................87
February 19—Maryland 29	Carolina....................22
February 21—V. P. I. 23	Carolina....................41
February 22—Navy 33	Carolina....................43
February 24—Davidson 10	Carolina....................19
March 3—S. I. C. Tournament,	
University of Georgia 26	Carolina....................17

Summary

Games won......10   Games lost......10

BASKETBALL 1930

CONTRASTED with Tar Heel basketball teams of the past two college generations, the 1930 University quint certainly cannot be termed successful. But the squad, tremendously handicapped because of graduations last June, made the most of mediocre prospects to finish the season with 10 wins and 9 losses. The Tar Heels showed a reversal of form in the last five games of the season, winning four of them by good margins immediately preceding the S. I. C. tournament in Atlanta.

Marpet
Guard

The Tar Heels finished the season in a tie for second in the Big Five League in North Carolina, but were eliminated from the Southern Conference tournament by Georgia in the opening round. For the first time since the inauguration of the tournament the White Phantoms were entered as "dark horses," but, after maintaining a 10-8 lead at the half, lost to the Georgia Bulldogs, 26-17.

Lacy Harper, elongated Tar Heel center from Pittsboro, was elected honorary captain for the 1930 season as it ended. Coach Jim Ashemore appointed a captain prior to each game, as none had been elected at the beginning of the season.

Brown
Guard

The Tar Heels had no outstanding individual contenders for the mythical All-Southern five, but Artie Marpet, captain-elect, was almost unanimously picked as a guard on the All-State quint. Marpet was hailed as one of the strongest guards at Carolina in recent years, and led the Tar Heels in scoring as well as floor work in several games.

Billy Brown, Tom Alexander, Bill Choate and others backed Marpet up at guard, while Neiman, Dameron, and Green were the most outstanding forwards. Harper was ably supported by Edwards at center, while on several occasions Dameron was shifted to this position.

Several pre-season games with Y.M. C.A.'s of the State were played by the Tar Heels. A loss to the Raleigh Y was the only defeat of the pre-season schedule, while wins were recorded over Durham, High Point, and two over Greensboro.

The season opened for the Tar Heels on January 11th, when they lost a two-point, 22-20, game to the Davidson Wildcats. A close, hard-fought game featured the meet with the 'Cats, and the two-point margin was

Harper
Center

a hard loss. The Tar Heels evened up the series with Davidson, however, when they met them again in the last game prior to the Conference tourney, in a 19-10 win.

Guilford and the Charlotte Monograms were played in succession after the Davidson game, and proved easy wins for the Tar Heels. Guilford losing 49-20, while the Charlotte Monograms took the small end of a 23-19 score.

In the first game with W. & L. at the "Hill' the Phantoms bowed before a superior General attack, 39-24. The Generals made a clean sweep of the state, defeating Carolina, Duke and State. Later the W. & L. quint were runners-up for the S. I. C. title at Atlanta.

Wake Forest and N. C. State were the next two Tar Heel victims. The Demon Deacons lost a one-sided affair 49-18, but the State quint was barely nosed out, 27-25, in Raleigh. On the return game with the Wolfpack in the Tin Can, the Techman nosed out the Tar Heels by another two-point margin, 28-26.

The opening game with Duke proved a one-sided defeat for the Phantoms in the Tin Can, 36-14, but the return game at Duke was more closely contested. The closest game the Tar Heels lost of the season was to the Blue Devils in Durham in the latter part of Febru-

Dameron
Forward

ary, 37-36. The results of this game hung in the balance until the final whistle. The Tar Heels and Devils exchanged the lead five or six times before the game ended, and a long shot from the floor placed the Duke quint in the lead as the whistle blew. Dave Neiman was high scorer of the evening with 22 points.

On the Northern trip the Tar Heels won and lost two contests. The tour opened with a win over V. P. I., 30-21, when Johnny Green led the Tar Heel scorers to win by a spurt in the last half which made the Tar Heels easy victors. W. & L. won their second game over the White Phantoms for the first Carolina loss of the trip, 27-17. The Virginia Cavaliers bowed before their Carolina rivals, 40-37, in a hard-fought game. Maryland closed the Northern campaign for the Tar Heels by winning, 36-33.

A Loyola rally in the closing minutes of play featured a one-point Tar Heel loss to the Chicago quint in the Tin Can, 26-25.

The Tar Heels won four out of five last games of the season prior to the Southern Conference tourney. Defeats over Wake Forest, and V. P. I. brought the total to two wins over these teams, while a victory over Davidson evened up the score with them one all. The win over the strong Navy quint showed a complete reversal

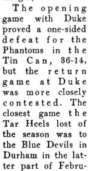

Neiman
Forward

Greene
Forward

Alexander
Guard

of form from the Tar Heels early season starts, and the game ended with midshipmen anchored on the lower end of a 43-33 score. Maryland accounted for their second Tar Heel win, 29-22, when they met at College Park.

The season ended with the Tar Heels recording 10 wins and nine losses, but an additional defeat at the hands of the Georgia Bulldogs in the S. I. C. tourney evened up the won and lost for the Carolina quint, 10 all.

The newly installed heating system of the Tin Can accounted for a large increase in the gallery which followed the Tar Heels dispite a season of mediocre success. The lack of seasoned veterans was felt keenly by the Carolinians, but the rookies rounded out fast, and showed flashes of championship form during the season.

Artie Marpet was perhaps the most outstanding individual player, but he was closely followed by Dameron, Neiman, Brown, Alexander, and Harper. Harper, the honorary captain, was injured in the final Duke game and thereby hindered his chances for any mythical All-State honors. Tom Alexander, playing his first year on the Varsity, showed

Edwards
Center

flashes of excellent form and was one of the steadiest of the Tar Heel guards. Billy Brown gave him a close race for the honors in this position. Dave Neiman's point gathering ability was clearly demonstrated in several games, especially in the Duke contest, where he garnered 22 points out of the Tar Heels total. Sandy Dameron was one of the most versatile of the Tar Heels, playing as center and forward with equal ability.

The season ended with the Tar Heels recording 10 wins and nine losses, but an additional defeat at the hands of the Georgia Bulldogs in the S. I. C. tourney evened up the won and lost for the Carolina quint, 10 all.

Cleland
Forward

Freshman Basketball

The Tar Baby basketball team had what might be called a very successful season. Their schedule consisted of games with all the Freshman teams in the Big Five of the State, and with the leading Freshman and prep school teams of Virginia. Although the team did not win every game played, it won the majority of its games, and was ranked among the leaders in the State. Much varsity material is expected from this team.

Choate
Guard

**1929
CAPTAIN
HENDERSON**

**1930
CAPTAIN
NIMS**

1929 Track Squad

TRACK 1929

Coach Fetzer   Coach Ransom   Manager Gray

Coaches _____"BOB" FETZER *and* DALE RANSOM

Captain _____JOHN HENDERSON

Manager _____BOWMAN GRAY

The 1930 Schedule

March 28—N. C. State at Chapel Hill.

April   5—Georgia Tech at Chapel Hill.

April   9—Duke at Chapel Hill.

April 12—Tech Relays at Atlanta.

April 19—Penn State at Chapel Hill.

April 21—V. P. I. at Blacksburg.

April 26—Penn Relays at Philadelphia.

April 28—Washington & Lee at Chapel Hill.

May 2-3—State Meet at Greensboro.

May 10—Princeton at Princeton.

May 16-17—Southern Conference Meet at Birmingham.

Nims

Barkley

Harper

Cowper in Action

Smith and Barkley Exchange
Batons

Track

Due to the diligent labor of Coach Fetzer and Coach Ransom and to the conscientious co-operation of the team, the Tar Heels were again able to uphold their reputation for excellency in track athletics. In fact, the 1929 track season may well be called one of the most successful in the history of the University. All meets, except the Southern Conference Championship, were won and won by large margins. Henderson, Nims, Neiman, Adkins, Gay, Harper, and many others proved to be stars of no little ability.

The season began on March second with the first annual indoor meet which was held in the "Tin Can." However, due to the fact that the visiting colleges were unable to send more than a minimum number of entrants, the team scores of this contest were not counted, but the Tar Heels succeeded in capturing many first places and no small number of seconds and thirds.

The regular outdoor season began with a dual meet with the Virginia Polytechnical Institute on April sixth. Carolina again showed brilliant form by winning a seventy-nine to forty-seven point victory. Gay, Harrison, Captain Henderson, Perry, Stafford, Harper, Neiman, and Bagby proved

Cowper

Henderson

Gay

Stafford

Neiman

Smith

their worth by winning first places in their various events. On April thirteenth, North Carolina upset some carefully thought-out dope by crushing Washington and Lee with a seventy-two and one-half to fifty-three and one-half victory. It was of still greater importance due to the fact that Captain Henderson and three other valuable men were in Atlanta for the Georgia Tech relays. In this contest with Washington and Lee two new University records were established: Adkins hurled the shot forty-two feet and five-eighths inches, and Neiman broad-jumped twenty-two feet and five and one-fourth inches. On Saturday, April twentieth, Carolina ran roughshod over Georgia Tech by defeating them ninety to thirty-six. In this meet the victors won twelve out of the possible fourteen first places, and Cowper established a new University pole vault record by clearing the bar at twelve and one-half feet. Four days later, Duke felt the effects of the Carolina onslaught by losing to the Chapel Hill team thirty-three and a half to ninety-two and a half. This was Carolina's most complete victory.

On May fourth, the Tar Heels went to Greensboro for the state championship meet. This contest, they won with a total of sixty-five and eight-

Nims Wins His Race

Stafford Broad Jumps in Duke Meet

Adkins

Perry

Harrison

Bagby   Garrett

Stafford and Perry in High Hurdles

Carolina Sweeps the 440-Yard Run

tenths points. Davidson was the next highest score with a total of thirty and five-tenths points. For Carolina: Gay took first place in both sprints. Cowper and Neiman won first and second honors in the pole vault. "Puny" Harper won the discus with a throw of one hundred and thirty-six feet and three inches, which established a new state record. The mile-relay team won their event by running the distance in three minutes and twenty-eight seconds.

The pick of the South's track men gathered at Birmingham on May seventeenth, for the annual Southern Conference meet. It was a cold rainy day, and the track was dotted here and there by pools of water. Everywhere it was wet and soggy. Due to this unfortunate circumstance, no records were broken, however, the times and distances were very good. The title was captured by Louisiana State University with a total of thirty-five points. Nevertheless North Carolina was close at their heels with a total of thirty-two and one-half points, only two and one-half points behind. This was the seasons only tragedy.

At the banquet that was held a few days after the close of the season, Dave Nims was elected captain, ensuing year.

Cox   Brown   Baucom

**1929
CAPTAIN
LUFTY**

BASEBALL

SCORE BOARD

INNINGS	1	2	3	4	5	6	7	8	9	10	11	12	R	H	E
CAROLINA	0	0	1	0	0	2	0	1					4		
VIRGINA	0	0	0	1	0	0	1	0	0				2		

**1930
CAPTAIN
MAUS**

[867]

BASEBALL 1929

Coach ....JIM ASHMORE

Captain ...."NAP" LUFTY

Manager ....JOHN BULLUCK

ach Ashmore   Manager Bulluck

The 1930 Schedule

—

March 27—Springfield, here.
March 28—Springfield, here.
March 31—Cornell, here.
April   1—Cornell, here.
April   3—Washington and Lee, here.
April   4—Georgia at Athens.
April   5—Georgia at Athens.
April   8—Maryland, here.
April 11—Maryland at College Park.
April 12—Virginia at Charlottesville.
April 14—W. & L. at Lexington.
April 15—V. M. I. at Lexington.
April 16—V. P. I. at Blacksburg.
April 19—V. M. I., here.
April 21—Davidson at Salisbury or Winston-Salem.
April 22—Davidson at Davidson.
April 23—Georgia, here.
April 24—Georgia, here.
April 25—V. P. I., here.
April 26—Duke, here.
April 28—Davidson, here.
May   3—Wake Forest, here.
May   6—State, here.
May   7—South Carolina, here.
May   9—Virginia, here.
May 10—Virginia at Greensboro.
May 12—Wake Forest, here.
May 17—Duke in Durham.
May 20—State, here.

BASEBALL 1929

Coxe

Satterfield

Whitehead

THE 1929 baseball squad may, for several reasons, be regarded as one of the most deserving clubs ever to represent the University. From the standpoint of games won and lost the Tar Heels were very successful with a record of only six losses out of a total of twenty-one games played. The team captured the honors of the Southern Conference Tri-State League, as well as gaining a tie with Virginia for the League trophy which must be won three times before a team gains possession of it.

The Tar Heels ushered in the baseball season by defeating the Springfield Y.M.C.A. College outfit in two successive games.

The University of Penn was next entertained. After two hard played games the Heels rested as victors. Next was the Easter Monday classic at Salisbury with Davidson. Lefty Ball pitched a winning game and the hard fought battle resulted in a 4 to 2 victory for Carolina in their first engagement away from the home lot. Next day Penn State stopped over to give the Heels their second of the four consecutive games of Easter-week. The game resulted in a neat victory for Carolina.

The third game of the week was with Cornell. This was the first club

Rand   Ball   Maus

to break our winning streak, which she did to the tune of 12 to 3.

The W. & L. Generals were our guests on Thursday. Five hits and a sacrifice in succession counted four runs for the Heels. With such a lead, Jim Ball rocked along in fine style with the entire team in support, to a 7 to 5 victory.

The Maryland club was our next dish. Wright soon had the Old Liners eating out of his hand. The Heels bunched their hits in the second, for four runs and in the fifth for three more, winding up with a 7 to 1 victory.

The first engagement on the Northern invasion was with the Old Liners at College Park. Carolina kept its Tri-State League record clean with a 6 to 4 victory over the Maryland Club.

Phil Jackson's homer enabled us to trounce the Old Liners for the second time this season.

Meeting Virginia for the first of the three game series to be played between the two institutions, the Carolinians came out with a dearly bought victory, 5 to 4. The Cavaliers took the lead but Carolina came back to crash through to a win. The Northern trip was successfully brought to a close by a victory over W. & L. at Lexington, the second of the season, and by victories of 8-2 over V. M. I. and V. P. I.

Ball hurled Carolina to a 4 to 2 victory over V. M. I. on Emerson Field on the 20th, Maus's triple in the eighth began the rally which ended the triumph and our eleventh victory of the season.

Barnhart   Lufty   Jessup

Coach Ashmore's charges continued their victorious march by winning over State in a terrific battle. The Heels nosed the Wolfpack out in the last few minutes to a 6 to 5 win.

Next on the programme was the V. P. I. Cadets. They were reported to have a formidable club, but the mighty Heels finally won out to the tune of 10 to 9.

Carolina then invaded the Devil's den at Durham. The Tar Heel team put up a strong fight but was crushed by the score of 9 to 6. This was the first game it had lost of the season to any college in the state.

We were again humiliated, allowing Wake Forest to win by a 4 to 3 score.

The Carolina cohorts then rallied, trouncing the Virginians for the sec-ond time straight with the long end of a 6 to 4 score. Satterfield led the hitting with 4 hits out of 5 times at bat.

The following day the Tar Heels victoriously wound up the series with 4 runs to Virginia's 2 in the annual game in Greensboro. Captain-elect Maus took three out of three to lead the batting.

For the second time straight this season the Devils trounced the Varsity. "Lefty" Jenkins, Duke Ace, pitched his team to a neat 8 to 5 win, giving the Carolinians a stinging humiliation.

The State game at Raleigh was rained out, and our next and final effort was with the Wake Forest Deacons.

This final game was painful to Carolina. The Deacons took the lead and kept it, winding up with a 7 to 2 victory.

1930
CAPTAIN
ALLEN

1931
CAPTAIN
GOODRIDGE

BOXING 1930

Goodridge

Sheffield

Coach ....CRAYTON ROWE
Captain ....ARCHIE ALLEN
Manager ....HERMAN SCHNELL

The Season

January 18—Washington & Lee................2   Carolina................................5
January 25—V. P. I. 2   Carolina................................5
February 1—V. M. I. 3   Carolina................................4
February 4—Duke University 2   Carolina................................5
February 8—Virginia 3   Carolina................................4
February15—Florida 5   Carolina................................2
February 17—South Carolina 1   Carolina................................6
February 22—Penn State 6   Carolina................................1
March 1-2-4—S. I. C. Tournament at Charlottesville.

Summary

Meets won 6   Meets lost........2

Allen

BOXING 1930

Koenig

Davis

DUE to its rapid increase in popularity at Carolina boxing was raised to a major sport following the completion of the 1930 season. The 1930 mitmen completed a hard 8-meet schedule against some of the strongest Southern and Northern teams with 6 wins and 2 defeats. Captain Archie Allen, undefeated, and Noah Goodridge, with only one loss to his credit before the S. I. C. Tournament, accounted for the individual Tar Heel honors by fighting in the finals of the Southern Conference Meet in Charlottesville.

Florida and Penn State accounted for the only two Tar Heel defeats. Florida succeeded Carolina to the Southern title, while Penn State was regarded as having one of the strongest teams in the country.

Washington & Lee opened the Tar Heel schedule by losing 5 to 2 at Lexington. Victories over V. P. I. and V. M. I. followed in quick succession.

Before one of the largest crowds of the season, approximately 2,000 or more, Duke was defeated 5 to 2 in the Tin Can.

A win over Virginia was closely followed by a defeat at the hands of Florida. Allen and Warren won by knock outs for the only two Tar Heel points.

With Capt. Allen not entered, Goodridge won the only Tar Heel bout against Penn State by defeating Casoni.

In the Southern Conference tournament Goodridge and Allen were the only two men to carry the Blue and White to the finals. They were defeated after putting up game fights and losing by close decisions. Carolina placed fourth in the meet.

Warren

YACKETY YACK

Captain Barkley
Cross Country

Captain Woodard
Wrestling

MINOR SPORTS

Captain Merritt
Tennis

WRESTLING 1930

Coach ....P. H. QUINLAN
Captain ....WAYNE WOODARD
Manager ....TOM HUNTER

Stallings   Woodard

The Season

January 25—Navy	22	Carolina	8
February 1—V. P. I.	13	Carolina	17
February 8—Princeton	15	Carolina	13
February 12—Davidson	12	Carolina	14
February 15—State	6	Carolina	24
February 22—V. M. I.	19	Carolina	9
March 4—Duke	8	Carolina	24

March   8—Southern Conference Meet at Lexington, Va.

Summary

Meets won.......4   Meets lost........3

Coach Quinlan   Manager Hunter

1929 CROSS COUNTRY SQUAD

CROSS COUNTRY 1929

Coach _____DALE RANSOM
Captain _____MINOR BARKLEY

FOR the fourth time in as many years the Carolina harriers annexed the Southern Conference title. Minor Barkley captained the Tar Heels to wins over Duke and State, and a loss by a small margin to V. P. I. However, in the Conference run in Chapel Hill the Tar Heels ranked first among the teams, with Lowery placing first for Carolina. This was the second S. I. C. cross country run at Carolina within the past 4 years.

Monograms were awarded to Barkley, Baucom, M. G. Cohen, J. Cohen, Lowery, Phoenix, Pierce and Wrenn.

Coach Ransom

Captain Barkley

1929 TENNIS TEAM

TENNIS 1930

Coach ....J. F. KENFIELD
Captain ....BILL MERRITT
Manager ....E. K. GRAHAM

. The Schedule

April 14—Alabama, here.
April 16—Davidson, here.
April 17—State Tournament, here.
April 18—State Tournament, here.
April 19—State Tournament, here.
April 21—Johns Hopkins, here.
April 23—Duke, here.
May   7—Davidson, there.
May   8—Vanderbilt at Nashville.

May   9—Sewanee at Sewanee.
May 10—Georgia at Athens.
May 12—Alabama, there.
May 13—Tulane at New Orleans.
May 14—L. S. U. at Baton Rouge.
May 15—Southern   Tournament   at
         New Orleans.
May 16—Southern   Tournament   at
         New Orleans.
May 21—Duke at Durham.

Coach Kenfield

Captain Merritt

[378]

1929 GOLF TEAM

GOLF 1930

Coach ....J. F. KENFIELD
Captain ....CHARLIE CHATHAM
Manager ....JUNE ADAMS

The Schedule

March 29—N. C. State, here.
April 9—William and Mary, here.
April 11—Wake Forest, here.
April 12—Duke, here.
April 19—Georgia Tech at Atlanta.
April 25—State Tournament at Greensboro.
April 26—State Tournament at Greensboro.

April 28—Vanderbilt at Nashville.
May 1-2-3—Southern Tournament at Birmingham.
May 10—N. C. State at Raleigh.
May 17—Virginia at Charlottesville.
(Duke and Wake Forest pending another engagement.)

1929-30 CHEER LEADERS

INTRAMURAL ATHLETICS

G. E. Shepard, Director

THE purpose of Intramural athletics is to provide some form of sport for all members of the student body. Director Shepard, assisted by "Mac" Gray, and Wallace Shelton, have kept this purpose steadfastly in mind and their efforts have resulted in the most successful year the Department has ever had. More students are participating in each sport every year, and additional events have been added to the Intramural program. Also more equipment has been provided by the Intramural officials. The slogan "Athletics for all" is becoming more and more a reality on the University campus.

THE TIN CAN—HOME OF INTRAMURAL SPORTS

Aycock Dormitory—Basketball Champions

Beta Theta Pi—Football Champions

Fall

TAG FOOTBALL:
Dormitory Champions........New Dorms
Fraternity Champions....Beta Theta Pi
Campus Champions........Beta Theta Pi

CROSS COUNTRY:
Team Winner................Tar Heel Club
Individual Winner ....T. Watkins

NOVICE TRACK MEET
Team Winner..................Beta Theta Pi
High Scorer ....D. Waugh

Winter

BASKETBALL:
Dormitory Champions................Aycock
Fraternity Champions ....D. K. E.
Campus Champions ....Aycock

Spring Program

Boxing   Tennis
Wrestling   Fencing
Track   Horseshoes
Baseball   Decathlon

1930 Fencing Squad

Beta vs. New Dorms

MONOGRAM CLUB

C. O. Sapp
J. D. McDaniel
R. S. Farris
C. M. Barkley
C. Wrenn
A. T. Allen
P. B. Abbott
C. E. Waddell
W. E. Merritt
W. L. Harper
F. A. Adkins
G. V. Cowper
D. A. Nims
J. S. Stafford
Philip Jackson
N. B. Lufty
R. R. Little
C. J. Blackwood
W. E. Eskew
C. P. Erickson
J. B. Fenner
R. M. Gray
J. T. Harden
H. C. House
J. S. Hudson
W. S. Koenig
J. E. Magner
J. R. Maus

E. S. Nash
C. L. Wyrick
C. R. Baucom
G. M. Cohen
W. G. Lowry
W. C. Medford
W. H. Brown
A. R. Harpet
Evan Vaughn
H. J. Sheffield
C. V. Cummings
Noah Goodridge
John Warren
G. O. Davis
L. F. Stallings
W. O. Woodard
R. H. Moore
Marion Cowper
F. J. Ferguson
Herman Schnell
M. D. Rand
B. U. Whitehead
Philip Sher
A. L. Wright
J. D. Bulluck
M. M. Shapiro
E. D. Yeomans
G. L. Bagby

E. P. Dameron
K. A. Gay
H. R. Garrett
David Neiman
W. A. Perry
Bowman Gray, Jr.
J. D. Branch
T. R. Brown
S. E. Crew
Gavin Dortch
E. D. Fysal
J. U. Gilbreath
E. R. Lipscomb
H. S. McIver
H. A. Nelson
R. A. Parsley
C. M. Redfern
F. W. Slusser
D. M. Snyder
L. A. Spaulding
G. D. Thompson
W. S. Tabb
J. K. Ward
D. J. Craig, Jr.
J. J. Cohen
C. B. Phoenix
G. N. Pierce
J. J. Alexander

ADVERTISING

Benjamin Franklin

FRANKLIN

Drive thy business! Let not it drive thee.
—POOR RICHARD'S ALMANAC.

Camels are odds-on favorites in every field. There isn't a cigarette . . . anywhere . . . that can touch them for fragrance, for mildness, for downright smoking *pleasure!*

Camel
C I G A R E T T E S

WOOTTEN

AND

MOULTON

Photographers

PORTRAIT
HOME PORTRAIT
COLLEGE ANNUALS
COMMERCIAL
PHOTOGRAPHERS

FORT BRAGG, N. C.
NEW BERN, N. C.
CHAPEL HILL, N. C.

[385]

THE TRUE ATMOSPHERE
of SCHOOL *and* COLLEGE

E endeavor, in producing school annuals, to render a helpful and constructive service directed toward enabling a student staff to get out a representative, distinctive book *within their budget.*

In connection with our new and modern printing plant we maintain a large Art and Service Department where page borders, cover designs, division pages, and complete decorative and illustrative motifs are created and worked out.

The
QUEEN CITY PRINTING COMPANY
Where Better Printing Costs Less
CHARLOTTE, N. C.

A COMPLETE SERVICE FOR SCHOOL PUBLICATIONS
PRINTERS OF THE YACKETY YACK